JOEL

Opening up
Joel

MICHAEL BENTLEY

DayOne

Michael Bentley has written an accessible and attractive devotional commentary on Joel—as straightforward and down-to-earth as the prophet himself!

Canon David Winter, former head of Religious Broadcasting at the BBC

In this volume Michael Bentley ably opens up the book of Joel with interesting observations, convincing explanations, challenging applications, and encouraging exhortations. This Minor Prophet's message must have a major impact on the life of any reader who carefully considers the clear narrative and ponders the probing questions which conclude each chapter of this little book.

Dafydd Hughes, Pastor, Grace Reformed Baptist Church, Palmerston North, New Zealand

When he preaches, Michael Bentley has the gift of drawing you in on a helpful and interesting journey of biblical understanding, insight and discovery. Michael's writing is no different, and this well-written and highly readable commentary on Joel will challenge and encourage you to go deeper with this prophet and with God.

Revd Alan Bradford, St Michael's Church, Warfield, Bracknell, UK

© Day One Publications 2010

First printed 2009

Unless otherwise indicated, Scripture quotations in this publication are from the New International Version (NIV), copyright ©1973, 1978, 1984, International Bible Society. Used by permission of Hodder and Stoughton, a member of the Hodder Headline Group. All rights reserved.

ISBN 978-1-84625-191-7

British Library Cataloguing in Publication Data available
Published by Day One Publications
Ryelands Road, Leominster, England, HR6 8NZ
Telephone 01568 613 740   FAX 01568 611 473
email—sales@dayone.co.uk
web site—www.dayone.co.uk
North American e-mail—usasales@dayone.co.uk
North American web site—www.dayonebookstore.com

All rights reserved
No part of this publication may be reproduced, or stored in a retrieval system, or transmitted, in any form or by any means, mechanical, electronic, photocopying, recording or otherwise, without the prior permission of Day One Publications.

Printed by Orchard Press Cheltenham Ltd.

*For Joshua Thomas Underwood,
my ninth grandchild, born 24 May 2009.
May he be strong and very courageous for the Lord.*

List of Bible abbreviations

THE OLD TESTAMENT

		1 Chr.	1 Chronicles	Dan.	Daniel
		2 Chr.	2 Chronicles	Hosea	Hosea
Gen.	Genesis	Ezra	Ezra	Joel	Joel
Exod.	Exodus	Neh.	Nehemiah	Amos	Amos
Lev.	Leviticus	Esth.	Esther	Obad.	Obadiah
Num.	Numbers	Job	Job	Jonah	Jonah
Deut.	Deuteronomy	Ps.	Psalms	Micah	Micah
Josh.	Joshua	Prov.	Proverbs	Nahum	Nahum
Judg.	Judges	Eccles.	Ecclesiastes	Hab.	Habakkuk
Ruth	Ruth	S.of S.	Song of Solomon	Zeph.	Zephaniah
1 Sam.	1 Samuel	Isa.	Isaiah	Hag.	Haggai
2 Sam.	2 Samuel	Jer.	Jeremiah	Zech.	Zechariah
1 Kings	1 Kings	Lam.	Lamentations	Mal.	Malachi
2 Kings	2 Kings	Ezek.	Ezekiel		

THE NEW TESTAMENT

		Gal.	Galatians	Heb.	Hebrews
		Eph.	Ephesians	James	James
Matt.	Matthew	Phil.	Philippians	1 Peter	1 Peter
Mark	Mark	Col.	Colossians	2 Peter	2 Peter
Luke	Luke	1 Thes.	1 Thessalonians	1 John	1 John
John	John	2 Thes.	2 Thessalonians	2 John	2 John
Acts	Acts	1 Tim.	1 Timothy	3 John	3 John
Rom.	Romans	2 Tim.	2 Timothy	Jude	Jude
1 Cor.	1 Corinthians	Titus	Titus	Rev.	Revelation
2 Cor.	2 Corinthians	Philem.	Philemon		

OPENING UP JOEL

Contents

	Background and summary	9
❶	Invasion of locusts (1:1–4)	11
❷	A warning to drunkards (1:5–7)	17
❸	Everyone is affected (1:8–12)	23
❹	A call to repentance (1:13–14)	29
❺	The day of the Lord (1:15–20)	36
❻	Warning notes of danger (2:1–11)	42
❼	Another call to repentance (2:12–17)	54
❽	The joy of restoration (2:18–27)	61
❾	A spiritual transformation (2:28–32)	69
❿	The nations judged (3:1–8)	76
⓫	Prepare for war (3:9–16)	82
⓬	Blessings for ever (3:17–21)	88
	Endnotes	95

8

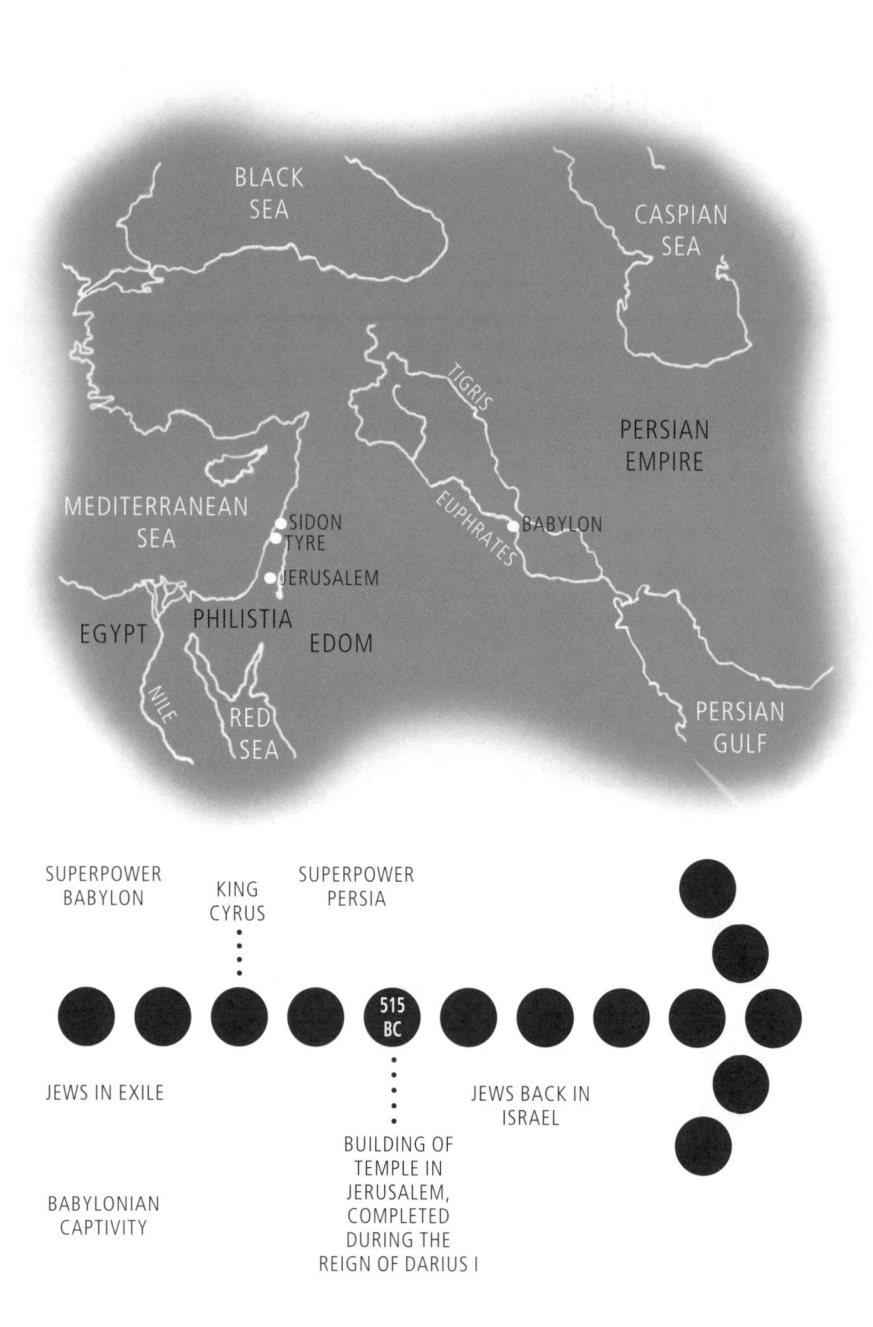

BLACK SEA

CASPIAN SEA

MEDITERRANEAN SEA

TIGRIS

EUPHRATES

PERSIAN EMPIRE

SIDON
TYRE
JERUSALEM

BABYLON

EGYPT

PHILISTIA

EDOM

NILE

RED SEA

PERSIAN GULF

SUPERPOWER BABYLON — KING CYRUS — SUPERPOWER PERSIA

515 BC

JEWS IN EXILE

BABYLONIAN CAPTIVITY

BUILDING OF TEMPLE IN JERUSALEM, COMPLETED DURING THE REIGN OF DARIUS I

JEWS BACK IN ISRAEL

OPENING UP JOEL

Background and summary

How did the Old Testament prophets know what to preach and write about? Did they study the earlier Scriptures and then think about how they could amplify them, or were these prophecies their own ideas? Certainly each of the prophets was steeped in the earlier writings and traditions that had been handed down from their forefathers. Without doubt, they meditated on these Scriptures and were convinced that God had spoken, and was still speaking, through them. Like Joel, many of the prophets described the source of their message in very simple terms: 'the word of the Lord ... came' (Joel 1:1). In other words, these were not just wise opinions about life; they were messages given directly to the prophets by revelation from God so that they could pass them on to the people of those days—and also to subsequent generations.

Who was Joel?

The only things we know about Joel for certain are written in this prophecy. He was 'the son of Pethuel' (1:1). There are twelve people in the Bible called 'Joel' but none of them can be identified as our prophet with any certainty. We know nothing about his father, either, but as Judah and Jerusalem are referred to several times in his prophecy (2:32; 3:1, 6, 8, 16–20), it is reasonable to assume that Joel and his family lived and worked in that area. The name 'Joel' means 'the Lord is God'. He may well have been a priest, because he spoke about ritual fasting and prayer and also referred to the elders and priests as important leaders in the community.

One of the ways to understand the meaning of any Old

Testament book is to see how it is used in the New Testament. Yet, although this book contains a very powerful and important message, there is only one direct quotation from it in the New Testament: in Acts 2:16–21, when Peter declared that the incredible events of the day of Pentecost were the fulfilment of Joel's 'day of the LORD' (Joel 2:28–32).

When was the book written?

There is nothing specific within the book to tell us when it was written. Although there are no identifiable historical events mentioned, both Greece (3:6) and Egypt (3:19) were obviously powerful nations at this time. However, because the compilers of the Old Testament placed the book very near the beginning of the twelve so-called Minor Prophets, many believe that it was written in the ninth century BC, before the deportation of the northern kingdom of Israel and the exile of Judah. Others conclude that it was compiled at a much later date—in the sixth century, after the return of Judah from exile in Babylon, and after the prophecies of Haggai and Zechariah. Yet there is nothing either within or outside the book to point more definitely to one of these periods of time rather than the other.

1 Invasion of locusts

(1:1–4)

Like the other prophets, Joel was concerned about 'the coming of the great and dreadful day of the LORD' (2:31). One of the signs that this day was drawing nearer was the arrival of a massive plague of locusts and the subsequent severe draught that afflicted the land of Judah.

God's judgement (vv. 1–3)

Everyone knew about this plague because it affected them all. The first thing God called Joel to do was to summon the elders of the people to 'Hear this' (1:2), because God was going to speak pointedly and with force.

The leaders of God's people have a very special responsibility to listen to the Word of God. Certainly pastors and elders today must take note of national and local events, but, more importantly, they are required to listen to the message of God's Word and act upon it. They should not merely delight in God's Word of blessing for their own benefit; they also have a duty to pass it on and explain it to others.

God's voice was not just for the elders; 'all who live in the land' had to pay heed to what God was saying. They were reminded that nothing like this had happened before in their own day or in the times of their forefathers. Furthermore, they were told to tell their children of these events so that they, in turn, could pass this message on to those who came after them (v. 3). Although the effect of these locusts was bad news, it paved the way for the good news that repentance would lead to salvation. Similarly, in the New Testament we read that Paul told Timothy to remember what he had said and then to pass it on (2 Tim. 2:2).

For Jews today, the Passover meal is still very special. At the beginning of the meal, a child asks four questions concerning why this night is different from all others. The story of the first Passover meal is then told. This good news is passed on to successive generations every year at this special feast.[1]

In Joel 1:3, however, the news that had to be passed on was not about joy and deliverance but God's coming judgement. So often people ignore bad news, thinking that, if they take no notice of it, perhaps it will go away. But bad news should not be disregarded; this plague of locusts was a message from God. The fact that it was not pleasant was no reason to take no notice of it. Its message was that God hates sin and that therefore everyone must seek to root it out of their lives and thoughts. Sin eats away at our whole being—mind, will and heart. Just as the locusts devoured everything within their path (v. 4), so our sin will eat away into our souls until we are as devastated as the land of Judah after the invasion of those destructive insects.

Sin seeks to destroy us. One of the ways we can defeat sin is by turning away from it. Organic farmers, who abhor the use of chemicals on their land, have turned back to natural ways to remove the weeds that choke their crops. One very effective method is to starve the weeds of the light, air and nutrients they need in order to grow. It is the same with sin. If we 'feed' the sin in our lives by succumbing to its attractions, it will grow stronger and stronger each day. The only way to kill it is to turn away from it with a strong desire to get rid of it.

> If we 'feed' the sin in our lives by succumbing to its attractions, it will grow stronger and stronger every day. The only way to kill it is to turn away from it with a strong desire to get rid of it.

That is why God sent the locusts on the land. The people had sinned, and were continuing to do so. The only way they could be brought 'to their senses' was by God descending upon them in this very powerful and memorable way.

The locust devastation (v. 4)

The plague of locusts is like the 'text' for this prophecy, yet they are only mentioned directly twice, in 1:4 and 2:25. However, their effect was a powerful sign of God's severe disapproval of the people's sin.

I well remember one particular morning in 1954, when I was serving at RAF Eastleigh in Nairobi, Kenya. All of a sudden, the sky darkened dramatically and all I could see was a moving mass of flying insects which looked like myriads of giant grasshoppers. They quickly moved away and left an eerie and stunned silence. That was my only experience of a locust swarm; later, I was told that it was just a small one.

From Joel 2:25, we can see that these swarms of locusts came yearly and wrought severe destruction upon the land. Joel 1:4 gives a very graphic description of them. The King James Version of the Bible speaks of the 'palmerworm', 'locust', 'cankerworm' and 'caterpillar', but the New International Version merely mentions 'great locusts' and 'young locusts'. The Hebrew uses four different words for these locusts, but it is generally thought by scholars that they are not four distinct kinds but four stages in the life-cycle of the locust.

The point to notice is the way in which verse 4 is constructed. It describes the completeness of the destruction of the crops. Similarly, the plague of locusts described in Exodus 10:13–15 'devoured all that was left after the hail—everything growing in the fields and the fruit on the trees. Nothing green remained on tree or plant in all the land of Egypt.'

Some commentators have concluded that these locusts are merely symbols of the invading forces of the enemies of God's people, but most agree that they were real locusts sent by God as punishment for the sins of the people. They were sent to warn them to return to the Lord in repentance. Thomas J. Finley writes of this event, 'Today the people need to contend with locusts; tomorrow they may have to suffer woes of the Day of the Lord.'[2]

From time to time, natural disasters come upon countries. In the summer of 2007, the UK was afflicted by severe floods. They started in the north of the country and then, a few weeks later, large numbers of people living in the West Country and parts of Wales were forced to leave their homes. Many items of furniture were damaged beyond repair and houses were left without electric power or water supplies.

There are few people like Joel around today to tell us whether or not this is God's judgement upon our land, but these events are surely warnings for us to take care and beware of the effects of our sinful lifestyles.

For further study ▶

FOR FURTHER STUDY

1. Why is it important to teach children the Scriptures? (See Exod. 10:2; Ps. 71:18; 2 Tim. 1:5.)
2. Joel uses the plague of locusts to indicate God's judgement upon the land. What can we learn about God's judgements from other Bible passages concerning locusts? See Exodus 10:4–6, 14–15; Deuteronomy 28:38; 1 Kings 8:37; Amos 4:9; 7:1.
3. Some natural disasters are sent or allowed by God to bring people to confess their sin and come to repentance. Note these natural disasters in the Bible: Amos 8:9; Luke 23:44–45; Habakkuk 3:6; Matthew 27:51–52.

TO THINK ABOUT AND DISCUSS

1. How should we explain to nominal Christians that attending church occasionally is no guarantee of salvation? (See Isa. 2:10–12; Jer. 4:6; Amos 5:18–20; Zeph. 1:7–8.)
2. Have there been times in your life when unexpected troubles, perhaps even disasters, arose? How did you deal with them? What did you learn from them about yourself and about God's dealings with you?

2 A warning to drunkards

(1:5–7)

There are times in our lives when we need a wake-up call. Too easily we become settled, take our luxuries for granted and behave as though it is our right to do whatever we want. Joel 1:5 begins with these startling words: 'Wake up.' Perhaps when we were children, this needed to be said to us by our schoolteachers, as our minds had drifted off during the lesson.

If we receive a phone call informing us that a loved one has been involved in a serious accident, we do not simply sit idly, musing upon the event; we jump into action. If we find water starting to pour through our bedroom ceiling, we don't stay lying in bed; we jump up to find the source of the problem and deal with it.

Joel's call to 'Wake up' is a technique used by many of the prophets. Amos pronounced 'Woe' to those who were complacent in Zion (Amos 6:1), and Zephaniah said he would search Jerusalem with lamps to warn those who were self-righteous (Zeph. 1:12). Sometimes a stirring call is suddenly shouted, but, at other times, the plea is gentler. Always the intention is to bring the people back to the ways of God. Throughout his little book, Haggai constantly called the people to 'give careful thought' to their ways (Hag. 1:5, 7; 2:15, 18). In Lamentations 3:40, we find a similar challenge with the call, 'Let us examine our ways and test them, and let us return to the LORD'.

To demonstrate the disastrous effect of these locust swarms, Joel likened their invasions to attacks by wild animals (v. 6). Those comparatively small locusts wrought so much havoc that it was as though a lioness (the vicious hunter among a pride of lions) had attacked and murdered the people with her powerful fangs. This was immediately followed by the proud male lion, which advanced and with its sharp teeth consumed the choicest part of the meat, leaving it bare, physically and morally. This, indicated Joel, is what God had made happen to the disobedient people of Judah.

The wake-up call to those immediately affected (v. 5)

It is sad, but often true, that people take no notice the first time they are warned of danger. The second and subsequent threats are frequently ignored as well. We have already seen that there is every indication that the locust attacks came with some regularity. Joel used these assaults as a tool to urge the people to realize the danger they were in through their lustful lifestyles; they had forsaken the Lord their God and had turned to other gods.

Every single individual living in the land would have been affected by the onslaught of these devouring insects.

Therefore, Joel urged them all to heed the call to repent of their many sins. Some people would have been aware of the ravages of these insects earlier than others, but, strangely, Joel mentions only one group in connection with the locust attacks: the drunkards. Lloyd Ogilvie comments, 'This group may be blind to the present distress because of their intoxication, but they will be wide awake when their supply of wine is exhausted without any to replenish it.'[1]

I know from my own childhood the great unhappiness that drunkenness can bring. My father, like many of the other workers in the small town in which we lived, did not earn very much money, but well over half his weekly wage was wasted on 'the horses' and 'the drink'. My mother had to run the household and pay all the bills out of the meagre sum my father gave her each Friday before he went off to the pub to get drunk with his mates.

Many of Britain's town centres are frequently plagued by young people who have drunk too much alcohol. They are not only noisy but destructive, causing many thousands of pounds' worth of damage to property, themselves and their drunken friends. On Friday and Saturday nights, police forces need to keep many men and women on duty just to keep order, and ambulance crews are called in increasing numbers to take youngsters to hospital solely because of drunken fights that have caused injuries.

Drunks often create as much noise with their raucous laughter as with their loud weeping. The drunkards in Joel's time were exhorted to 'wake up', 'weep' and 'wail'; their longed-for 'new wine' had been snatched from their lips, because the locusts had eaten all the grapes from which the wine would normally have been made.

Although Joel would certainly have been concerned about the bad behaviour of the drunkards and the sadness brought to their families, he was much more anxious because of the danger that these locusts symbolized. That peril was the threat of invasion by the dreaded Assyrians.

Attacks upon God's possessions (vv. 6–7)

These verses speak of the Lord's loss. He tells of 'my land', 'my vines' and 'my fig-trees'. Similarly, the first verse in chapter 2 tells us that Zion is also his: 'my holy hill'. We sometimes forget that 'the earth is the LORD's, and everything in it' (Ps. 24:1). The people of Joel's time should have remembered that the Lord had given them this land (Deut 1:25; Josh. 1:2–3) but, even so, it still belonged to the Lord. We speak of 'our' houses and land but, in fact, these have only been lent to us. When we are called upon to leave this earth we do not take them with us. We may 'will' items to our children or other people, but they will not own them for ever; the land and 'our' possessions all belong to the Lord.

> We speak of 'our' houses and land but, in fact, these have only been lent to us. When we are called upon to leave this earth we do not take them with us.

The major possessions of the people of Joel's day were their crops. Vines and fig-trees often grew in the same fields, and these hungry, invading locusts 'laid waste' the vines and 'ruined' the fig-trees—even stripping off the bark. This is similar to how bored youngsters, and others, often behave in our town centres today. They wreak havoc on anything that is wholesome because their drunken or drug-induced stupors lead them to smash and destroy things that are not their own. As the locusts are hungry for food, so these people are hungry for anything that will distract them from life and its challenges.

Sometimes the branches of dead trees turn white. These are like the 'whitewashed tombs' that Jesus speaks of in Matthew 23:27; they might look strangely beautiful on the outside, but on the inside, there is nothing but death. Often, the bark of trees is knobbly and hard. This is because it is made up of dead cells. When these were alive, part of their purpose was to protect the inner bark (the phloem). Bark is designed to transport 'food' from the leaves to other parts of the tree, including its roots. However, when all the bark is stripped off the tree, there is no hope left for it.

This was the prospect that awaited God's people (v. 7); and it was solely because they had turned aside from following the Lord who loved them and had given them their home.

It is a blessing that Joel did not finish his prophecy at this point.

For further study ▶

FOR FURTHER STUDY

1. Israel did not own the land; to whom did it really belong? See Leviticus 25:23; Psalm 24:1; Jeremiah 2:7; 16:18; Ezekiel 36:5; 38:16; Joel 3:2.
2. What do fruitful vines and fig-trees represent in the Old Testament? See 1 Kings 4:25; Micah 4:4; Zechariah 3:10.

TO THINK ABOUT AND DISCUSS

1. What signs do you see in the world today that the Lord is calling all people to repent of their sin?
2. Have there been times in your life when you have been forced out of your comfort zone to act quickly to deal with an issue? What did you learn from those experiences?
3. How should we treat land and those who inhabit it? Read, for example, Exodus 20:8–10; Deuteronomy 22:6–7; 24:19–22.

3 Everyone is affected

(1:8–12)

When trouble comes to a family, it is not only the members of the immediate household who are affected; its repercussions reach their neighbours and friends. Similarly, when a nation is attacked, those who suffer are not just the people living in the immediate area; the consequences spread like ripples on a lake after a stone has been thrown into it.

When the plagues of locusts ravaged Judah, it was not only the drunkards who felt the effect; everyone suffered. Although the drunkards wept and wailed because they were soon going to be deprived of their drink, others suffered because the fields were ruined.

This section of Joel is written in the present tense. Judah was urged to mourn like a bereaved virgin. Then Joel gave a list of disastrous things that were happening in the land ('Grain offerings ... are cut off', 'The fields are ruined', etc.).

These things would lead to much mourning, despair and an absence of joy.

The virgin mourns (v. 8)

The first illustration is that of a virgin who is looking very cast down. She is dressed in very uncomfortable and unglamorous sackcloth because she has lost her husband, because he has either died prematurely or been killed—possibly in battle. If she is mourning for her 'husband', why is she described as a virgin? It was the custom in those days that, once an engagement had been announced, the couple were regarded as man and wife, even though there was no sexual relationship until after they were officially married.

We can imagine the deep sorrow which overwhelms this virgin. For many months or even years, she has been looking forward with great excitement to the moment when she will be given to her husband and they will become one flesh. For her, there will have been no possibility of a career in business because her one burning ambition has been to devote herself to pleasing her husband and bringing up their children. However, since his early death, all those longed-for aspirations have suddenly died and there is little or no hope for her in widowhood. She is just as lifeless as the fig-trees which have been stripped of their bark and whose branches stand like ghosts in the moonlight because of the attacks of the locusts (v. 7).

Most of Joel's hearers would have seen this as a picture of the deprivations they were passing through. The more spiritual people would also have realized that the prophet was warning the nation of their danger. Just like the virgin in Joel's picture, God expected much—of his people—yet the only fruit they had produced was religious adultery (i.e. they had worshipped false gods rather than the true and living God). This adultery could only lead the whole nation into spiritual deadness.

> God expected much—of his people—yet the only fruit they had produced was religious adultery

The priests are frustrated (vv. 9–10)

Next, Joel brought the situation of the priests to the attention of the people. What were they to do? Their main task was to offer sacrifices to God on behalf of the people and to seek atonement for their sin, yet the drought that followed the plague of locusts had left them without any grain, wine or oil to use for their daily offerings. Their offerings had been 'cut off from the house of the LORD', so it is no surprise that the priests were mourning the loss of their work just as the virgin grieved over the loss of her husband. Without the means of offering sacrifices, what service could they perform?

Today, most people in the West would not be concerned in the slightest if their religious leaders were unable to perform their duties, but things were different in the nation of Judah, which was God's own possession. The fact that the priests were unable to perform their tasks affected everyone.

In verse 10, Joel reminded the people of their ruined fields that had produced nothing. The wheat that earlier in the year had begun to germinate and sprout had been destroyed by the drought. This disaster had also dried up the possibility of new wine, and there was a lack of olives from which oil ought to have been pressed. Grain, new wine and oil were vital for temple worship, as Exodus 29:38–41 and Numbers 28:3–8 tell us. The 'grain moistened with oil and a libation of wine accompanied the morning and evening burnt offerings of lambs'.[1]

Today, many countries have a shortage of rain, bringing great difficulty to the people, but the more pressing problem is the absence of spiritual refreshing, just as it was in the days of Joel. Amos warned his hearers of the coming days when there would be 'a famine of hearing the words of the LORD' (Amos 8:11). For many people, these dry days are with us now. In 1772, William Cowper wrote this moving hymn:

O for a closer walk with God,
A calm and heavenly frame,
A light to shine upon the road
That leads me to the Lamb!

Farmers are despairing (vv. 10–12)

Farmers were the next to be highlighted. Like the virgin and the priests, they too were in despair, because 'The fields are ruined, the ground is dried up; the grain is destroyed, the new wine is dried up, the oil fails' (v. 10).

Harvest time was always a cause of great rejoicing for the people of Judah (Ps. 4:7; Isa. 9:3). But now, because of the devastation caused by the locusts and the deadness resulting from the drought, all happiness had flown away. The farmers, who all year had waited for their crops to mature and produce a harvest, were wailing like the virgin and the priests. The failure of the wheat, barley, pomegranates, palms and apples was compounded by the lack of grain, wine and oil (vv. 11–12). Everything was dried up, and 'Surely the joy of mankind is withered away'.

This was a sad commentary on the state of the people's hearts. They found no enjoyment in their Lord because their hearts had been dried up by sin, and, perhaps, because they still adhered to false religion. Yet, despite their sin, they were not entirely bereft because God still had his eye upon them. He had sent his servant to call them to repentance and a better way of living. In the next chapter we will see some of the duties the Lord required of them.

For further study ▶

FOR FURTHER STUDY

1. What does the Bible picture of marriage teach us about our relationship with God? See Isaiah 54:5; Jeremiah 3:14; Hosea 2:19–20; Ephesians 5:23–24.

2. Study the following Bible passages regarding the wearing of sackcloth when mourning for the dead: Genesis 37:34; 2 Samuel 3:31; Isaiah 3:24; 22:12. In what ways should we express our grief for our sinful behaviour?

TO THINK ABOUT AND DISCUSS

1. Have there been times in your life when your hopes and aspirations were suddenly and unexpectedly dashed? How did you react? How should Christians react in such situations?

2. How would you explain to a Christian couple that sex before marriage is unbiblical and sinful?

3. Sometimes the ministry at your church or home group may seem very dry. Are there things that you could do to help bring some spiritual life into such situations?

4 A call to repentance

(1:13–14)

The whole population of Judah was suffering because of the damage caused by the invasion of the locusts and the severe drought that followed. Yet, although the people were in great distress, they had little concept of the real issue—they had sinned, and sinned grievously.

Up to this point, Joel's vivid words have described the dire situation without giving any hint of the reason for the trouble; now he jumps right to the heart of the matter and issues a call to repentance.

The priests (v. 13)

First Joel addresses the priests. They were the religious leaders of the people. Because of their calling and duties they ought to have been close to God and therefore aware of the people's sin. It was their responsibility to offer daily sacrifices in the temple (i.e. they represented the people to God), and also to remind the people what God required from them (i.e. they spoke on behalf of God to the people). The priests should have known of God's anger over the people's sin. However, they appear to have so focused their minds on their temple work that they had failed to notice that the people had drifted away from the true God and, worse still, had turned to the worship of other gods.

Their temple work should not have taken up so much of their time and energy that they failed to notice how the people were behaving. Their concern about temple worship was no excuse for failing to ensure that the people were loyal to their God. Their actions were similar to those of the priest and the Levite in the parable of the Good Samaritan (Luke 10:25–37).

How many pastors today are so involved with vital work like preparing sermons and talks, participating in social action within the community or attending meetings, that they do not notice that the people under their spiritual care have grown cold towards their Lord? Church leaders have the solemn responsibility of ensuring that the people continue to follow the Lord closely, both outwardly and in their inner spiritual lives.

Throughout the whole of Judah's—and Israel's—existence, the people had been locked into a downward spiral of sin. When Moses disappeared into the cloudy heights of Mount Sinai, the people got impatient waiting for his return and wanted some object to worship, so they pleaded with Aaron to make them a golden calf. They quickly forgot all that God had done in rescuing them from the horrors of Egyptian slavery and keeping them safe on their journey through the desert.

At the end of their forty-years' desert wandering, the Lord commanded them to remain separate from the Canaanites and the other heathen nations who were their neighbours in the Promised Land. Sadly, when they finally arrived after their long journey, they cast eager glances in the direction of the fertility gods of these other nations and longed to enter into the sexual excitement of the worship of the Baals and the Asherah poles. This visible heathen worship, with its desire to increase fruitfulness, was much more attractive to them than the worship of a God they could not see (and who might, or might not, grant their wishes). They longed for the freedom to worship the gods of these other nations and to be like their neighbours. They forgot that the word 'different' lies at the heart of the concept of 'holiness'. Similar things happened in the days of the judges. Great things were accomplished during the time of Gideon, but 'No sooner had Gideon died than the Israelites again prostituted themselves to the Baals' (Judg. 8:33).

Time and time again the people sinned and followed these other gods, but again and again the Lord graciously sent his prophets to bring them back. Sometimes they listened, repented and returned to the Lord—but their 'repentance' only lasted for a limited time. Not many years passed before the same kinds of sin gripped them again and they were dragged down into idolatrous behaviour. It is no surprise, then, that God called both Israel and Judah 'faithless' and described their behaviour as adulterous (Jer. 3:6–9). Jeremiah had to tell the people that 'They have returned to the sins of their forefathers ... They have followed other gods to serve them.' God declared that 'Both the house of Israel and the house of Judah have broken the covenant I made with their forefathers' (Jer. 11:10).

In most of the Minor Prophets we find references to the people having turned away from the Lord to serve other gods, but in the book of Joel there is no direct mention of idolatry; there is a hint of it when Joel describes how Judah would behave if they did repent: 'Then you will know that I am in Israel, that I am the LORD your God, and that there is no other' (2:27). In other words, Joel said to them, 'If you cease trying to find satisfaction in serving other gods and turn back to the Lord, you will discover that the Lord is not just an almighty God; he is the *only* God—and he is alive and will bring judgement on sinful people.'

> If you cease trying to find satisfaction in serving other gods and turn back to the Lord, you will discover that the Lord is not just an almighty God; he is the *only* God—and he is alive and will bring judgement on sinful people.

These priests, more than anyone else, ought to have been aware of the people's sinfulness, so Joel calls them to 'wake up'. He then orders them to 'put on sackcloth', 'mourn' and 'wail'. As we have seen, 'Sackcloth was worn in biblical times as a sign of both mourning and penitence … The custom was to wrap the sackcloth around the loins, with the upper body of males left bare. This was in order that the chest might be struck in grief, which is the meaning of mourn in v. 13a.'[1] Not only were the priests to dress in uncomfortable sackcloth during the day, they were also required to 'spend the night in sackcloth'. There would be no part of day or night when they could take off these itchy garments, a constant reminder of the pain caused to God by their sin.

The elders and the whole population (v. 14)

The priests were also required to 'Declare a holy fast; call a sacred assembly'. In 1:2, the elders and 'all who live in the land' had been called upon to consider the devastation of the locusts. Now Joel urges the priests to summon 'the elders and all who live in the land to the house of the Lord your God, and cry out to the Lord'.

This custom goes back to the original Day of Atonement, when the whole nation was called upon to seek cleansing from the pollution of their sin. In Leviticus 23:27–29 we read that 'The tenth day of this seventh month is the Day of Atonement. Hold a sacred assembly and deny yourselves, and present an offering made to the Lord by fire. Do no work on that day, because it is the Day of Atonement, when atonement is made for you before the Lord your God.' This was followed by a solemn stipulation: 'Anyone who does not deny himself on that day must be cut off from his people.'

Although it was not the time of year for the annual Day of Atonement, the calamity in Judah was so great that Joel entreated everyone to fast and seek the Lord's forgiveness without delay. We have other examples of solemn fasts being held in addition to the official Day of Atonement. When Samuel called upon the people to return to the Lord, he first commanded them to get rid of their 'foreign gods and the Ashtoreths'. When they had done this, he called them to assemble at Mizpah, where he promised to intercede with the Lord on their behalf. 'On that day they fasted and there they confessed, "We have sinned against the LORD"' (1 Sam. 7:3–6). We cannot hope for God to forgive us unless we first forsake our sin and then humbly and sincerely demonstrate that we are truly repentant and desire to serve the Lord wholeheartedly.

The Puritans were very wise in making sure that their gospel preaching started from the premise that people need to recognize the heinousness of sin and then repent of it.

FOR FURTHER STUDY

1. Hebrews 12:1 tells us that sin 'so easily entangles' us. Starting with the worship of the golden calf in Exodus 32, study the Bible passages that show how the Israelites subsequently turned away from God and his law.
2. Look at Judges 20:26; 2 Samuel 1:12; 12:16–23; Ezra 8:21–23. What do we learn about fasting and mourning in Old Testament times? How does this relate to our need to confess and depart from sin in our day?

TO THINK ABOUT AND DISCUSS

1. Think about those times when you have drifted away from God, either openly or secretly in your heart. How did God bring you back into fellowship with himself?
2. How can we firmly adhere to the teaching of the Word of God and yet be good citizens in these days when 'tolerance' demands that one person's opinion is treated as of equal value to that of somebody else? How do you cope with the demands of society when they fly in the face of the clear teaching of God's Word?

5 The day of the Lord

(1:15–20)

Joel now called upon the elders, who were secular leaders, and all the people to turn aside from their sin; without genuine repentance, their fasting would be pointless. This call was vital and urgent. His voice was very stern as he cried out, 'Alas for that day! For the day of the LORD is near; it will come like destruction from the Almighty' (v. 15).

The people would have known about 'the day of the LORD'; it was a concept known in Israel from the time of the judges.[1] In those days, God was seen as their Almighty Lord who fought for and with his people against their enemies (see Josh. 10:11; 24:7; Judg. 5:4–5), but the Minor Prophets saw things slightly differently. They did not view the day of the Lord as one on which Israel triumphed over their enemies; rather, it was the reverse.

Perhaps Amos was the first of the Old Testament prophets

to emphasize the solemn aspect of the day of the Lord. He informed the people that the day of the Lord would not bring light to the people, but darkness (Amos 5:18–20). Zephaniah (1:1–18), Isaiah (2:6–22), Ezekiel (7:1–27) and Malachi (3:1–5; 4:5) take up the theme in a similar way.

This day would not be a minor irritation; it would 'come like destruction from the Almighty'. The words translated 'destruction and 'Almighty' sound similar in the original Hebrew. Therefore, 'the Almighty' could also be rendered 'the Destroyer'.[2] Isaiah and Ezekiel use very similar words to describe this same day (see Isa. 13:6; Ezek. 30:2–3).

Many of the events that take place in the world today are frightening, but they are merely a foreshadowing of that final day of the Lord—the day of judgement that will come upon the whole world. Both Jesus and Paul refer to this day. On that day, everyone will be forced, not merely exhorted, to stand before God's judgement seat (Matt. 12:36; Rom. 14:10).

This is one of the reasons why Joel stressed the urgency of repentance. The Rich Fool, in Jesus's parable, said to himself, 'Take life easy; eat, drink and be merry.' He assumed that he had many years ahead of him and that, as many think today, 'when you're dead, you're dead, and that's the end of it'. However, this wealthy man came to see that he did not have a long life in front of him: God demanded his life that very night (Luke 12:16–19). None of us can afford to ignore God's warnings because 'that day' is going to be dreadful, and it is 'near' (Joel 1:15). Paul tells us, 'The hour has come for you to wake up from your slumber' (Rom. 13:11), and the Lord himself urged us to work while it is still day (John 9:4).

Signs of God's judgement (v. 16)

As we have seen, the drought and famine not only brought hardship to the ordinary people, it also affected the worship of the temple. It was stipulated that offerings were always to be accompanied by joy, yet the food had been 'cut off before our very eyes' (v. 16). Not only had they no food to offer, they had no joy to express, either.

The farmers (v. 17)

Seeds that had been sown with the hope of a harvest had simply shrivelled and died because there was no moisture in the ground to cause them to swell and germinate. Instead of the storehouses and granaries being filled with grain, they were empty and useless. The subsequent years would be even bleaker because there was neither food nor seeds to plant for successive crops.

The cattle (v. 18)

The plight of the land was echoed by the frightening 'moan' of the domestic cattle in their agony of hunger and by the furious activity of the herds as they milled about in their fruitless search for a few blades of grass to eat.

These animals are very resourceful when it comes to finding grass. They will even nibble down to the roots of plants in their search for food. In 2007, my wife and I went on a short trip to Jordan. In the summer, the southern part of the country is very brown; much of it is desert. Yet along the hillside we saw many large flocks of sheep and goats moving along in groups, with their heads down to the ground searching endlessly for what little sustenance they could find. The amazing thing is that these sheep did find something to fill their stomachs. Those of Joel's day were not so blessed. The food had been cut off so that 'even the flocks of sheep are suffering'.

Famine

Amos took a similar scene and prophesied, '"The days are coming," declares the Sovereign LORD, "when I will send a famine through the land— not a famine of food or a thirst for water, but a famine of hearing the words of the LORD"' (Amos 8:11). We still live in a day of famine so far as the hearing of the Word of God is concerned. In some churches, much is said about global warming, the plight of refugees and the needs of the persecuted, but little is heard about God's call for us to spend time and energy feeding on his Word.

Those of us who have the privilege of preaching God's Word or teaching in Sunday school or Bible study groups should not teach as though 'God is rather an agreeable deity largely devoted to helping us out of difficulties'.[3] Neither should we give the impression that sin is merely something that is 'socially unacceptable' or the result of 'poor environment, faulty parenting, inadequate schooling or the human propensity to occasionally make mistakes'.[4] Instead we should declare the Word of the Lord fearlessly.

A prayer for mercy (vv. 19–20)

Joel ended this first section of his prophecy by turning to God in prayer. He knew that the Lord would not desert his people, even though they were very sinful and disobedient to his law, so he cried out for mercy. Twice in this short prayer he stated that 'fire has devoured the open pastures'. In the Bible, fire is almost always a symbol of God's judgement—it is not just something that happens when grass is dry (see, for example, Gen. 19:24; Deut. 4:24; Josh. 7:15; Isa. 47:14; 66:15–16; Jer. 4:4; 5:14; Amos 7:4).

The wild animals of verse 20 are symbols to show that even dumb creatures have more sense than God's people. Isaiah 1:3 tells us that 'The ox knows his master, the donkey his owner's manger', but, sadly, 'Israel does not know, my people do not understand'. So Joel said, 'Even the wild animals pant for you', just as 'the deer pants for streams of water' (Ps. 42:1), but would the people search for God? Would they be genuinely sorry for their sins and seek repentance? Joel knew that they would not do so if they were left to their own devices, but he still called out to his God to have mercy upon them.

FOR FURTHER STUDY

1. See what the New Testament has to say about the day of the Lord or the day of Christ: Matthew 24:29–31; Mark 13:24–26; Luke 21:25–28; Romans 2:5–10; 1 Corinthians 1:8; 3:13; 5:5; 2 Corinthians 1:14; Philippians 1:6, 10; 2:16; 1 Thessalonians 5:2.

2. Study the way in which Joel uses the phrase 'the day of the Lord'. Sometimes it is a day of wrath against Israel (see 1:15; 2:1, 11) and sometimes against the nations (see 2:31; 3:14).

3. How is joy associated with worship throughout the book of Deuteronomy? See, for example, Deuteronomy 12:6–7, 18; 14:26; 16:11, 14; 26:11; 27:7.

TO THINK ABOUT AND DISCUSS

1. What would you say to someone who said that there was no need to repent because 'God loves me and everything will turn out all right in the end'? Which Bible verses would you use to back up your argument?

3. The storehouses in Joel's day were empty and useless. Have there been times when you have felt worthless or inadequate? How did the Holy Spirit fill you and send you out with God's power to achieve useful things for his glory?

6 Warning notes of danger

(2:1–11)

I started my school life just as the Second World War broke out. The first few months of the conflict came to be known as 'the phoney war', because everything seemed to carry on as it always had done—except that an uneasy stillness crept over the country. I sensed that everyone was extremely apprehensive.

One morning, we were suddenly startled by an eerie wailing noise coming from a factory chimney next to our school. We soon learned it was called 'the siren' and that, when it sounded, we needed to go to a place of safety. Similarly, Joel pleaded with the city authorities for a warning note to be sounded in Jerusalem.

Wake up! (v. 1)

In the name of the Lord, Joel demanded that those responsible for the safety of the people 'Blow the trumpet in Zion' and 'sound the alarm on [God's] holy hill'. This was to be no half-hearted, apologetic 'toot' but a strong and urgent blast. The prophet issued this call again at 2:15.

The trumpets of those days were made from rams' horns and their sound was nothing like the sweet music of today's orchestral trumpets; it was a juddering signal that an enemy was approaching the city.

Everyone knew that the Assyrians aimed to conquer the whole known world, but this did not worry the people of Jerusalem because they knew they lived in God's chosen city, the place of his dwelling. They could not envisage that an enemy could touch their beloved 'Zion'. They trusted in the strength of the Lord and also the mountains of Samaria to protect them (see Amos 6:1). However, this kind of thinking would prove futile.

Many Christians suppose that everything will go well with them because they go to church regularly and say their prayers fairly often. However, the Lord will not allow sinful behaviour to continue unabated; one day there will be a reckoning. Like today's Christians, some of the people living in Jerusalem should have taken heed of the clear teaching of God's Word.

In Deuteronomy 28, the Lord had spoken of the blessings in store for those who were obedient to his Word. He promised that he would set them 'high above all the nations on earth' (28:1) and that they would be 'blessed in the city and blessed in the country' (v. 3). But here in Joel we read about the devastation caused when the plagues of locusts and famine arrived. The Judeans may well have reasoned, 'How can a loving God change his mind?' But God had not changed his mind, nor was he capricious or vindictive. He is always the same and he keeps his Word. The inhabitants of Jerusalem had chosen to forget that those promises of God were conditional. He had said, 'All these blessings will come upon you and accompany you *if you obey the* LORD *your God*' (Deut. 28:2). The Judeans had not been submissive to him, and one of the penalties for disobedience was that they would sow much seed in the field but would harvest little because locusts would devour it (28:38).

With hindsight, it is obvious to us that these disasters would come upon them because they had worshipped 'other gods' (28:36). Therefore the Lord would bring 'a nation against you from far away, from the ends of the earth, like an eagle swooping down, a nation whose language you will not understand ... They will lay siege to all the cities throughout your land until the high fortified walls in which you trust fall down' (28:49, 52).

The message of Joel is that complacency must be banished from the thinking of God's people: all who lived in the land would 'tremble, for the day of the LORD is coming. It is close at hand' (2:1). The church also needs to remember that today is not a time to be sitting at ease. There is work to be done for the sake of the kingdom of God, but there are also warnings to heed. Cain was angry when God cautioned him, 'sin is crouching at your door; it desires to have you, but you must master it' (Gen. 4:7). A 'holy life' will not stop Satan from trying to lure

> **The message of Joel is that complacency must be banished from the thinking of God's people.**

OPENING UP JOEL

Christians away from the things of God. How many godly servants of the Lord have been tempted by 'the lust of [their] eyes' (1 John 2:16) and been drawn into unwise relationships with members of the opposite sex? How many pastors have proved to be unprofitable servants because they were 'puffed up with pride' and boasted of what they had achieved? Every Christian should pay attention to Paul's words to the Corinthian church: 'if you think you are standing firm, be careful that you don't fall!' (1 Cor. 10:12). There is no excuse for laziness in these days because the Lord has sounded his warning note that 'the day of the LORD is coming. It is close at hand'.

The day of the Lord (v. 2)

Four unpleasant words are used to describe the atmosphere on that awesome day. It would be 'a day of darkness and gloom, a day of clouds and blackness'. We associate these kinds of things with the night—the dark night of despair, sorrow and foreboding. Amos also told his hearers that the day of the Lord would be 'darkness, not light—pitch-dark, without a ray of brightness' (5:20). In a spiritual sense, darkness is a picture of people without God, because where the Lord is, there is light. He came into the world to bring light, but the people who were living in darkness did not understand (John 1:5).

Those without Christ and the blessings of the gospel will stumble and fall because their eyes have not been opened to see the glory and beauty of the Lord Jesus Christ. Yet Christians themselves also 'walk in darkness' when they choose to ignore, or disobey, the clear teachings of God's

Word. The people of Joel's time should have been ready for the approach of the enemy but they were lethargic. They did not believe they needed to worry about such things because God was with them and he loved them; they assumed that everything would turn out well for them simply because of who they were.

> Today, many Christians are sleepy. They are happy to belong to a church and sit through the services but they refuse to become active in the work of the gospel.

Today, many Christians are sleepy. They are happy to belong to a church and sit through the services but they refuse to become active in the work of the gospel. They would rather go to a party than to a prayer meeting. A concert excites them, but they see the conversion of the lost as nothing to be thrilled about. They will work hard on the grounds surrounding the church building, but pay little attention to their own growth in faith. They happily put a nominal amount in the offering bag, but they have no interest in offering themselves for the work of the Kingdom.

There is a great need for God's people in the 21st century to 'wake up'. The enemy is approaching. They may be so lethargic that they do not notice that Satan is like a 'roaring lion'; they have no awareness that he is 'looking for someone to devour' (1 Peter 5:8). Perhaps some Christians would rather stay in a darkened room all day so that their sinfulness will not be exposed by the light (John 3:20). However, these believers forget that the dawn is fast approaching and with it the penetrating light of God's glory, which will certainly probe into the tiniest nooks and crannies in their minds and souls.

A few years ago, my wife and I joined a small party of people touring the Sinai Peninsula in Egypt. It was still dark when we reached the peak of the mountain, but suddenly the first fingers of dawn shot over the edge of the mountain and then rapidly spread across the whole area so that soon everything was exposed to the sun's brilliant, piercing light.

Normally in Scripture, the coming of the dawn signifies the arrival of joy and gladness. Isaiah declares, 'your light will break forth like the dawn, and your healing will quickly appear' (Isa. 58:8), and Proverbs 4:18 tells us that 'The path of the righteous is like the first gleam of dawn, shining ever brighter till the full light of day'; but that is not the picture here. In Joel 2, the coming of the dawn signifies the swiftness of those enemies who would soon devour the land. Just as dawn spread rapidly across the mountains, so this large and mighty army of Assyrians, pictured as more locust swarms, would rapidly devour the land. It would be an army such as had never been seen before nor would be seen again in the future.

Every one of God's people today should learn from this. We must all be on our guard because the enemy of souls is likely to swoop at any time—particularly when he is least expected. Jesus himself continually warned us to

> We must all be on our guard because the enemy of souls is likely to swoop at any time—particularly when he is least expected.

be alert. He used the picture of a burglar when he said, 'If the owner of the house had known at what time of night the thief was coming, he would have kept watch and would not have let his house be broken into' (Matt. 24:43). Because of the attacks of the evil one, Paul urges us to 'Put on the full armour of God so that you can take your stand against the devil's schemes' (Eph. 6:11). We may think that we are ready for any attack from the enemy of souls but Satan uses subtle tactics—he attacks us at our most vulnerable point and when we are least expecting it. Proverbs 4:23 tells us, 'Above all else, guard your heart, for it is the wellspring of life.' Like dawn spreading rapidly across the mountains, our hearts can easily rule our heads so that, before we know it, we find ourselves slipping swiftly downwards into danger.

The speed of the enemy (vv. 3–5)

As we read this next section, our breath is almost taken away as the rapid advance of the invading army is depicted in highly poetic detail. Joel tells us what would happen 'before them' and 'behind them'. 'Before them' the hungry locusts would see a rich agricultural land, 'like the garden of Eden'; they would swoop down with the fire of God's wrath, and all that would be left behind would be 'a desert waste' (v. 3).

These 'locusts' would have 'the appearance of horses [that] gallop along like cavalry' (v. 4). The people of Jerusalem were reminded of the noise that chariots make as they charge down the hillsides into the homes of unsuspecting people. The crunching of numerous pairs of locust teeth resembled the sound of cracking fire as they consumed the stubble that had been left after the gathering of a harvest (v. 5).

In the years before the Second World War, the people of France felt very secure because, during the 1930s, they had built and patrolled the magnificent Maginot Line. This was supposedly an impenetrable barrier between France and Germany, built to ensure that France would not be overrun as it had been in the First World War. On 10 May 1940, however, Hitler's army bypassed the French defences and went north, marched through Belgium and swiftly sped through the whole of Western Europe. They were able to make such rapid progress because the German divisions were equipped with military tanks which had been developed during the First World War. When they came into use, they were called 'Iron Horses'. In 1940, these 'Panzer divisions' moved at tremendous speed as they conducted a lightning war (*blitzkrieg*) against Belgium, the Netherlands and France. Their advance was very reminiscent of the advance of the Assyrian army described in these verses by Joel.

The determination of the enemy (vv. 6–9)

Joel used the present tense as he warned the inhabitants of Jerusalem that they would see terrible devastation. They were brash in their dismissal of Joel's warning, but then they would be in anguish because of the sight of this powerful army. Everyone would turn pale as they realized the horror of the situation (v. 6).

The army would be highly disciplined. They would move forward like warriors marching into battle. Their cavalry charge would be gloriously spectacular. Walls would fail to stand in their way and nothing would divert them from their predetermined path. No one would break ranks, neither would there be unseemly jostling for position; 'each marches straight ahead'. When they reached the city, they would rush upon its walls and then swiftly run along them. However strong the houses of Jerusalem were, they would prove to be no barrier to these 'locusts', who would climb into them like burglars.

When our Commander-General, the Lord God Almighty, calls us onto the battlefield of this life, we should spring into battle and proceed to take our marching orders from him alone. When he gives his signal for action, we should not question it. Instead, we should move at his word.

So often, Christians fear the enemy of souls and take fright when they hear his 'roar'. However, God's people have nothing to be afraid of if they are obeying the orders of their Master and when Satan is 'bound' (Rev. 20:2). When we go out into the darkness of the world with the biblical weapons of evangelism, we should not be afraid of what the enemy can do to us.

Does an atheist frighten us? Is the soul of a sinner so blackened by years of iniquity that it seems to be impenetrable? Christians should not fear. The Lord says to us,

… do not fear, for I am with you;
do not be dismayed, for I am your God.
I will strengthen you and help you;
I will uphold you with my righteous right hand.
All who rage against you
will surely be ashamed and disgraced;
those who oppose you
will be as nothing and perish.

(Isa. 41:10–11)

The secret of their strength (vv. 10–11)

The assault of the enemy would not only make the citizens of Jerusalem tremble in fear; their rapid progress would also make the earth shake and the sky tremble. The vast numbers of 'soldiers' in this army would block out the light of the sun by day and the moon by night, and when it stormed the city, even the stars would be obscured (v. 10).

It is at this point that Joel revealed the identity of the commander of this invading army. We can image the incredulous surprise of the people of Jerusalem when they learned that it was their own Lord who 'thunders at the head of his army'. How could their foe be under the direction of the Lord? The answer was the same as that given through Zephaniah: 'The great day of the LORD is near'. Zephaniah added that it would be a 'day of wrath, a day of distress and anguish' (Zeph. 1:14–15), and this rage would be poured out upon God's own people. 'These things will come about for one reason only: "because they have sinned against the LORD" (Zeph. 1:17).'[1]

This frightened surprise will be merely a pale reflection of the alarm that will take place on the great day of the Lord that is still in the future for us. On that day, just as in the days of Joel, the Lord himself will 'thunder at the head of his army'. He will command his vast and mighty forces, which will be beyond number. Certainly these invaders are evil, but they obey the command of the Lord.

The prophet ends this section with the trumpet call, 'The day of the LORD is great; it is dreadful. Who can endure it?' Many of the prophets asked a similar question. This should not surprise us, because each prophet described the same 'day of the LORD'. Isaiah saw the invading Assyrians as the Lord's instruments (see Isa. 10:5–7; 13:4); Jeremiah understood the threat of the Babylonians in the same way (see Jer. 25:9; 43:10).

Our prophet cries out, 'Who can endure the day of the LORD?'; Nahum asks, 'Who can withstand his indignation? Who can endure his fierce anger?' (Nahum 1:6); Malachi wonders, 'But who can endure the day of his coming? Who can stand when he appears?' (Mal. 3:2); and John, in Revelation, speaks of the wrath of the Lamb, asking, 'Who can stand?' (Rev. 6:17).

A dire situation was facing the inhabitants of Jerusalem, and an even worse one faces all who continue in their sinful lifestyles. The Bible makes it clear: sin must be paid for. '[The] wicked man will die for his sin' (Ezek. 33:8), and the only way of escape from this punishment is for wicked men and women (and that includes many 'good' people) to 'turn from their ways and live' (Ezek. 33:11). Life is found only by turning to God and coming to him through his dear Son, the Lord Jesus Christ.

FOR FURTHER STUDY

1. What was the significance of blowing the trumpet in the following verses: Numbers 10:5–7; Judges 6:34; Jeremiah 4:5; 6:1; Ezekiel 33:3?
2. Read Matthew 24:33; Philippians 4:5; James 5:8; 1 Peter 4:7. What difference should the nearness of the Lord's Second Coming make to our lives?
3. Christians today are often slow to work together in evangelistic endeavours. What can we learn about unity in the gospel from the Scriptures? See Philippians 1:27; 1 Corinthians 16:13; Titus 1:9; Jude 3.

TO THINK ABOUT AND DISCUSS

1. What would you say if one of your friends said to you, 'I have plenty of time to think about religion. Don't bother me about that now'?
2. How could you use people's fear of the dark to speak to them about Jesus, the Light of the world?

7 Another call to repentance

(2:12–17)

The people of Judah must surely have been cowering under the hammer blows of Joel's warnings when he passed on God's declaration, 'The day of the LORD is great' (v. 11). They certainly could not ignore these words—particularly after the great calamity that had already descended on them through the swarms of locusts.

It would have been understandable if the Lord had turned his back on them. Yet, immediately following the solemn warnings of future judgement, he now speaks graciously to the people of Jerusalem and Judah. He tells them there is something they must do about their wickedness if they want to please God and avoid further punishment. They should return to the Lord in a sincere and unreserved desire to repent of their past waywardness.

Come back home (vv. 12–14)

When God said, 'Even now ... return to me', it was as if he was saying, 'Despite all your disobedience and forgetfulness of me and my laws, I am offering you the hope of mercy if only you will turn round, leave your sinful ways and come back to me with all your heart, mind and soul.' Amos said something similar when he called the people to 'Hate evil, love good' and 'maintain justice in the courts'. He then added, 'Perhaps the Lord God Almighty will have mercy' (Amos 5:15).

The people had been so selfish and stubborn that they could have turned their backs on this call to repent. This was to be no feeble, half-hearted coming back to God and his ways: the Lord's desire was that his people would return to him *'with all [their] heart'*. Because they had become so used to sinning, they would find it difficult to turn round and go back to God.

They would have discovered, as we do, that the human heart is 'deceitful above all things' (Jer. 17:9). That was why the writer to the Proverbs urges us to 'guard [our] heart' which is the 'wellspring of life' (Prov. 4:23). Paul took up this theme when he spoke of the need for God's people to 'Put on the full armour of God' (Eph. 6:11). The enemy of souls, the devil, will do all in his power to move us away from the things of God, but we will experience 'the peace of God, which transcends all understanding' when we turn away from self and centre our desires solely upon the Lord. He will then 'guard [our] hearts and [our] minds' because we are 'in Christ Jesus' (Phil. 4:7).

John Murray has a very helpful description of

repentance in his book *Repentance Accomplished and Applied*. He writes, 'Repentance consists essentially in change of heart and mind and will. The change of heart and mind and will principally respects four things: it is a change of mind respecting God, respecting ourselves, respecting sin, and respecting righteousness.'[1] This is not so easy as it sounds.

In Joel 2:16-17 the priests were urged to gather the people in the temple for a time of national repentance. This alone could bring the mercy which the Lord wanted to bestow upon his people.

> The act of repentance is not something that we can merely decide to do when we are feeling like it.

How can anyone actually come to the point where he or she repents—and does so wholeheartedly? The act of repentance is not something that we can merely decide to do when we are feeling like it. It requires a radical change wrought in our hearts, minds and wills by the Spirit of God.[2] Later in Joel 2 we are given the promise of the Holy Spirit, who will come in a new and mighty way (see 2:28-30). He is the one who gives us the desire and the power to turn to Christ in sincerity.

In our own experiences, we have probably come across people who have said 'sorry' to us when they have hurt us, but then very shortly afterwards they have gone back to their old ways. The Lord does not want his people to be like this. In his great psalm of repentance David understood that the sacrifices of God are 'a broken spirit' and that God does not reject those who come to him with a 'broken and contrite heart' (Ps. 51:17). Jeremiah spoke of the unfaithfulness of Judah in not returning to God 'with all her heart, but only in pretence' (Jer. 3:10).

When Joel urged the people to return to the Lord, he reminded them that 'he is gracious and compassionate, slow to anger and abounding in love' (2:13), repeating words spoken by God to Moses following the backsliding of the people in worshipping the golden calf (Exod. 34:6). We can hear the pleading in the voice of Joel as he longed that the people would have a change of heart. If they did, perhaps the Lord would withdraw from his anger, even at the eleventh hour, and grant them a token of his blessing.

The message of these verses is not confined to people of long ago living in Old Testament times. In the very first verse of Mark's Gospel we read, 'The beginning of the gospel about Jesus Christ, the Son of God', followed by a quotation from Isaiah about the messenger who would come before him, and then the words: 'and so John came, baptising in the desert region and preaching a baptism of repentance for the forgiveness of sins' (Mark 1:4). A few verses later we read the words of Jesus after John had been put in prison: 'Jesus went into Galilee, proclaiming the good news of God. "The time has come," he said. "The kingdom of God is near. Repent and believe the good news!"' (Mark 1:14–15). Following the outpouring of the Holy Spirit on the disciples on the Day of Pentecost, Peter preached to the people and they were 'cut to the heart' and cried out, 'Brothers, what shall we do?' Peter replied, 'Repent and be baptised, every one of you, in the name of Jesus Christ for the forgiveness of your sins' (Acts 2:37–38). This message of repentance is at the beginning and at the heart of any return to the Lord, but we should continually live a life of repentance because, sadly, we continue to sin.

God's glory must not be diminished (vv. 15–17)

The trumpet was sounded to prepare all the people for a 'holy fast' and 'sacred assembly'. No one was to be exempt from this gathering. The elders are mentioned first, then the children and those nursing youngsters. 'Only an extreme emergency would make a couple cancel their wedding plans.'[3] According to the Law of Moses, a man was exempt even from military service for a year after his wedding (Deut. 24:5), but here we see that even the bride and bridegroom were to leave their secluded and exclusive love-nests.

The priests were required not only to lead the people; they were also instructed to stand between the entrance to the temple and the altar of burnt offerings. As they ministered to the Lord, they also interceded for all the people. They were concerned about the welfare of the people but they were also uneasy because the honour of the Lord was at stake.

Earlier in their history, Moses had pleaded with God to spare the people from his anger. He was sorry, not so much for the people as for the Lord's honour. All the surrounding nations knew that the God of Israel had brought the Israelites out of Egypt's bondage; Moses argued with the Lord that, if he destroyed his people, 'Then the Egyptians will hear about it!' and would conclude that God did not have enough power to bring the people into the land he had promised to them (Num. 14:12–15).

In a similar way, when Nehemiah's efforts to rebuild the walls of Jerusalem were being threatened by Sanballat and his gang, he prayed, 'Hear us, O our God, for we are despised ... [The enemies] have thrown insults in the face of the builders' (Neh. 4:4–5). Nehemiah was rebuilding the city walls for the glory and honour of the Lord and those who tried to prevent this happening were dishonouring God. No one should be reticent to proclaim the name of the Lord. The psalmist prayed, 'Help us, O God our Saviour, for the glory of your name; deliver us and forgive our sins for your name's sake. Why should the nations say, "Where is their God?"' (Ps. 79:9–10).

Even though God's people have to suffer, they are still able to find peace in their afflictions. Paul and Silas were able to sing praises at midnight in prison while their limbs ached and their wounds festered (Acts 16:25). There is always a way back to God if only people will seek him. We all need to remember that God's Word says, 'Even now ... he may turn and have pity' (Joel 2:12, 14).

For further study ▶

FOR FURTHER STUDY

1. Repentance was often symbolized by the tearing of clothes (see Gen. 37:29; Num. 14:6; 2 Kings 22:11). How did this show their sorrow for sin, and what other ways are there of demonstrating true repentance?

2. From the following verses, what do we learn about the compassion shown by the Lord as he seeks to bring sinners to himself: Numbers 14:18; Psalm 86:15; Nehemiah 9:15; Hosea 11:8; Zephaniah 3:17?

TO THINK ABOUT AND DISCUSS

1. In the following Scriptures, how does God demonstrate that he is abounding in love: Exodus 34:6; Psalm 103:2–13; Micah 7:18–20? In what ways do you reflect God's love to others?

2. What actions can you take to steer yourself away from brooding on the misdeeds of others and feeling bitter at the way in which you have been treated?

8 The joy of restoration

(2:18–27)

This section starts with the word 'Then'; the implication is that the people of Judah would repent and would do so wholeheartedly. If they refused to return to the Lord, none of these benefits would be granted to them. These blessings would arrive in answer to the changed hearts of the people and the fervent prayer of the priests (2:17).

From the Ten Commandments we know that the Lord is 'a jealous God ... but showing love to a thousand generations of those who love [him] and keep [his] commandments' (Exod. 20:5–6). We see further evidence of the Lord's gracious and compassionate nature when he assured his people that he would take pity on them and respond positively to their prayer.

After the locust invasion, there was no food for the people and for the temple offerings, but now the Lord promised to send 'grain, new wine and oil' following increased rain. This would not be enough merely to keep them alive; it would be in such abundant quantity and quality that it would 'satisfy [them] fully'.

Although this prophecy was addressed to backsliding Judah, it also has relevance to the Christians of our day. We assume that the call to repentance is solely for those who have never known the joy of salvation, but we should remember that it is also necessary for believers to return to the Lord and to keep doing so regularly. Being filled with sorrow for sin is a foreign concept for Christians who have grown cold towards spiritual things. The inhabitants of Jerusalem were in a similar condition before Joel's message had its cleansing effect upon them. It is no surprise that the people in neighbouring countries had taunted them for worshipping a God who apparently had done nothing to help them in their distress. They had become a byword among the nations (2:17). However, Joel told them that, following their sincere repentance and prayers, they would 'never again ... [be] an object of scorn to the nations'.

God's dealings with their enemy (v. 20)

The people of Jerusalem might hear of wars and rumours of wars, but they did not need to be alarmed (see Matt. 24:6) because the Lord would take action on their behalf. He would drive their enemies (the northern army) far from them. The primary meaning was still the plague of locusts. Even though those insects would normally have come from the south, it was not unheard of for them to arrive from a northerly direction. Judah was now given the assurance that God would deal with this insect-horde and drive it into the desert regions, where, because there would be no vegetation for it to feed upon, it would wither and die. He would divide their teeming mob so that half of it ended up in the sulphur-ridden Dead Sea where nothing can live (the eastern sea) and the other half into the swirling waters of the Mediterranean Sea (the western sea). The dead bodies of this locust swarm would heap up in foul piles that would putrefy and cause a great stench to fill the air, just as happened with the bloated corpses of the Egyptian army lying dead on the seashore (Exod. 14:28–30).

A secondary meaning, however, refers to those aggressors from the north that were determined to invade and then destroy Judah. To the east of Jerusalem lay a great desert, and to the west was the Mediterranean Sea. Any invader could therefore only come from the south (Egypt being the major country situated in that direction) or the north. When the Syrians, Assyrians, Babylonians and Medo-Persians invaded Judah, they all marched from the north.[1] In uncompromising language, Joel informed the people that God would destroy this evil army so that, rather than the people of Judah being 'an object of scorn to the nations', it would be the invaders whose dead soldiers would form heaps of rotting flesh, causing a terrible smell. This would be the destiny of the northern invaders who believed they had 'done great things'.

Rejoice and be glad (vv. 21–24)

Judah was to be afraid no longer. Previously they had been

called upon to weep (1:5), mourn (1:8) and put on sackcloth (1:13), but once they repented, even the land itself was to rejoice (2:21). The animals were to be unafraid (v. 22) and the people were to be glad (v. 23). Their sorrow would be turned to joy (see John 16:20). They would not have deserved these blessings, but the Lord would shower his love upon them, solely because of his grace and goodness.

It never ceases to amaze me that God has shown his grace and goodness to me. When I have wandered astray, he has brought me back into his fold. When trouble has come upon me, he has always been there beside me. Sometimes I have said hurtful things to others, but even then he has poured in his oil of healing and eventually granted me peace.

The verses in this section remind us of many psalms of praise where we are exhorted to 'praise the Lord'. The 'great things' done by 'the northern army' would pale into insignificance in comparison with the 'great things' that the Lord would do for his people (v. 21). He had rescued them from the enslaving might of Egypt. He delivered them from all their enemies during their desert wanderings, and he led them into the Promised Land. Despite all those times when they backslid, he showed his loving-kindness towards them and brought them back to himself.

The enemies of God's people may have appeared to be stronger than the people of Jerusalem, but Judah did not need to be afraid. Instead, the people were to be 'glad and rejoice' because the same Lord who had done great things for them in the past would surely continue to do mighty works for them in the times of their great need in the future. Moses had told the Israelites, 'Do not be afraid or terrified because of [your enemies], for the LORD your God goes with you; he will never leave you nor forsake you' (Deut. 31:6). The locusts had afflicted the land, the animals and the people of Jerusalem, but the land was now to 'be glad and rejoice', the wild animals were to be unafraid and the people of Zion were to rejoice in the Lord their God (vv. 21–23).

Before their eyes, 'the open pastures [would become] green. The trees [would bear] their fruit' and 'the fig-tree and the vine [would yield] their riches'. This total change in their situation would happen because of the complete alteration in the behaviour of the people. God would demonstrate to everyone—even to those jeering nations around them—that he had forgiven his people by sending his 'autumn rains in righteousness' and 'his abundant showers, both autumn and spring rains, as before' (v. 23).[2] This would result in the threshing-floors being filled with grain and the vats overflowing with new wine and oil.

An abundant restoration (vv. 25–27)

The Lord then promised to do something even more incredible. The people would not merely go back to the situation they were in before the locusts arrived; incredibly, all the 'fruit' that they lost during those years of devastation would be restored to them. Those wasted years of harvest would be restored by an abundance of bumper crops. They might have thought about those awful days (recorded in 1:4) and the bitterness left to them through the destruction caused by the various-sized locusts, but all their losses would be paid back.

This news must have gladdened the hearts of the people.

Instead of being exhausted by the trials of the past, they would be able to take up their agricultural tools with rejoicing. They would not have to work twice as hard to fill their storehouses to the level they should have been at before the locusts arrived. The Lord would give them every piece of grain, fruit and oil they would have had in their stores if the plague had not come upon them. They would have plenty to eat until they were full. They would enjoy a double quantity of the Lord's blessings. They would give praise to the name of the Lord, for he had worked wonders for them (see v. 21). But there was more: they would be given the assurance that never again would they be shamed (v. 27).

Those of us who have gone astray from the Lord's paths often grieve because of the wasted years of our empty lives, but in Joel the promise is that the Lord will repay you for those years of emptiness. This was the pattern set by the Lord in ancient Israel. 'If a man steals an ox or a sheep and slaughters it or sells it, he must pay back five head of cattle for the ox and four sheep for the sheep' (Exod. 22:1; see also Lev. 24:18).

> Nothing will be achieved by living with regrets.

Nothing will be achieved by living with regrets. Those who return to the Lord will find that he has returned to them and given them fresh vigour to labour in his service. They may not be able to put the clock back and live the former years all over again, but they will be able to have fresh zeal for the honour of the Lord. O. Palmer Robertson says, 'Living with regrets is sin for a Christian. Regret is the sorrow of the world that works death. Living with regret has nothing to do with the godly repentance that leads to life and restoration. Living with regret means that you refuse to believe the glorious truth that God restores the years that the locusts have eaten.'[3]

When we live for God we will know that we are not battling on our own. The people of Judah were not only given the promise of God's presence; they were also told, 'Then [after they had returned to the Lord] you will know that I am in Israel, that I am the LORD your God, and that there is no other' (v. 27). For the first time in this book there is mention of Israel. It seems that this was a reminder to the people of Jerusalem that they were not on their own. The Lord was not only the God of Judah, but the God of the whole of Israel (including the northern part of the kingdom).

How important it is to know for certain that the Lord is our own God as we face the enemies of this life! When Moses went back to Egypt to lead the Israelites out of slavery, God appeared to him and instructed him, '… say to the Israelites: "I am the LORD, and I will bring you out from under the yoke of the Egyptians … I will be your God. Then you will know that I am the LORD your God' (Exod. 6:6–7). Our God is no myth, despite the claims of Dr Richard Dawkins' best-selling book *The God Delusion*. He is not like man-made wooden idols that 'know nothing', 'understand nothing' and whose 'eyes are plastered over so that they cannot see, and their minds closed so that they cannot understand' (Isa. 44:18). Our God has been revealed to us in and by the Lord Jesus Christ. When we believe in him, his light shines in our hearts. He has given us 'the light of the knowledge of the glory of God in the face of Christ' (2 Cor. 4:6).

For further study ▶

FOR FURTHER STUDY

1. Why should God grant his blessings to unworthy people? Think about the teaching of the following passages and write down or discuss your wonder at such goodness: Deuteronomy 7:7–9; Romans 5:6–8; Ephesians 2:1–10. Perhaps you could write a hymn, poem or a piece of prose on the undeserved favour of God.

2. Study the following psalms: Psalm 40; 95; 145. What has God done that causes the psalmist to praise him? Can you praise him for similar things?

TO THINK ABOUT AND DISCUSS

1. If you had the ear of the leaders of your country, what would you say to urge them to turn back to the Lord? (See Deut. 32:15; Ps. 14:1–3; Isa. 1:4–6; Jer. 23:14.)

2. How would you counsel a distressed Christian who had returned to the Lord from a time of backsliding and was deeply distressed about his or her wasted years away from God and the people of God? (See Ps. 32:1; 103:3–4; Isa. 55:6–7; Hosea 6:1–3; Rom. 2.4.)

9 A spiritual transformation

(2:28–32)

Everything would improve. In 2:25 God had promised to restore the lost years caused by the locust invasion. Now he assured the people of Judah of even greater blessings.

These greater blessings were things that would happen 'afterwards' (v. 28). The 'before' was full of disaster and the loss of basic essentials for life, but the gloom and despair of those days were going to give way—first to material blessings and then, 'afterwards', to an abundance of spiritual grace. These would be amazing wonders that could not have been envisaged while the people were in the midst of their trials.

When the people had repented wholeheartedly (vv. 12–17), there would follow an abundance of rain that would enable bumper crops to grow (vv. 23–24). Everything that the people of Judah had lost would be recovered (vv. 25–26). However, these things were only the beginning of God's provision. Far, far greater blessings were to come.

God's Spirit will be poured out on all people (vv. 28–29)

When Moses was feeling very discouraged because the work

of leading the people was getting too onerous for him, he was advised to appoint seventy elders to help him. The Lord promised to take the Spirit that was in Moses (i.e. God's Spirit) and put that same Spirit into these seventy elders (Num. 11:17). When Joshua raised concerns because two of them were prophesying, Moses said, 'I wish that all the Lord's people were prophets and that the Lord would put his Spirit on them!' (Num. 11:29).

Similarly, when David was anointed king over Israel, 'the Spirit of the Lord came upon David in power' (1 Sam. 16:13). Saul, David's predecessor, also had the Spirit of the Lord upon him, but later God's Spirit left him (see 1 Sam. 16:14). It is only when we come to the written prophets that we read of the permanent promise of God's Spirit. Ezekiel promised that God would put a new spirit within his people (Ezek. 11:19), and Jeremiah spoke of the coming days when God would make a new covenant with his people (Jer. 31:31). These same promises were detailed more clearly by Joel, through whom God said that 'afterwards' (or 'the days are coming when') 'I will pour out my Spirit on all people' (v. 28).

The 'afterwards' came hundreds of years later. Luke tells us that, on the Day of Pentecost, after the crucifixion of the Lord, a group of about 120 followers of Jesus 'were all together in one place' (see Acts 1:15; 2:1).

> Suddenly a sound like the blowing of a violent wind came from heaven and filled the whole house where they were sitting. They saw what seemed to be tongues of fire that separated and came to rest on each of them. All of them were filled with the Holy Spirit and began to speak in other tongues as the Spirit enabled them.
>
> (Acts 2:2–4)

The Holy Spirit did not descend and come into them; he was 'poured out' upon them, just as Joel had prophesied. The Spirit was given in such measure that each of the disciples was completely transformed. Before that incident, they were scared stiff and afraid to admit their adherence to Christ for fear of being arrested and hung on a cross as he had been; but then the Holy Spirit came upon them with such a mighty force that they were no longer afraid. Instead, they were filled with boldness and given an overwhelming desire to declare Christ to all the people. They now had no hesitation in reminding the Jews that it was they who had put Jesus to death, but that God had raised him up to life again.

> The Spirit was given in such measure that each of the disciples was completely transformed.

After Pentecost, the abundant outpouring of God's Spirit was no longer reserved for people like kings and prophets. The promise in Joel was that all people would be eligible to receive God's Spirit. Some might argue that Peter's quotation of Joel 2:28–32 in Acts 2:17–21 meant that only the Jews would receive the Spirit. Certainly the phrases 'your sons and daughters … your old men … your young men … my servants, both men and women' could be seen as applying exclusively to Judah, but verse 32 makes it abundantly clear that the message went much further afield. It was for 'everyone who calls on the name of the LORD', and the assurance given is that they 'will be saved'.

But does this mean that everyone will be saved in the end? No, because this is not the teaching of Scripture. Writing about Mammoth Hot Springs in the Yellowstone National Park, USA, Theo Laetsch stated, 'A thirsty man may stand at the brink of Mammoth Springs and die of thirst if he refuses to drink water. A man may be offered the full measure of the Holy Spirit and his sanctifying power; he will remain in spiritual death and die eternal death if he refuses, rejects, this gift.'[1] When the Bible states that 'everyone who calls on the name of the LORD will be saved', it means that all those who call in faith, believing on the name of the Lord Jesus Christ, will be delivered from hell. This does not mean that grace is only available for those who feel so frightened that they call on the Lord to have mercy on them. Throughout the Old Testament, we find that it was those who acknowledged that the Lord was their God who 'called upon him'. During the days of Seth 'men began to call on the name of the LORD' (Gen. 4:26), and Abram 'built an altar to the LORD and called on the name of the LORD' (Gen. 12:8).

The diverse types of people to whom this blessing was promised must have been surprising for Joel's original hearers. Not only sons would prophesy, but daughters too. It is true that most of the people who are named as prophets in the Bible were men, but Anna is described as a 'prophetess' in Luke 2:36, and Acts 21:9 tells us that 'Philip ... had four unmarried daughters who prophesied'. Paul takes up this teaching and tells us that there is no distinction of age, sex or social class when it comes to receiving the Spirit of God (Gal. 3:28).

Another way in which God would communicate was through dreams. Joel said, 'you old men will dream dreams, your young men will see visions.' 'Throughout the Old Testament we find God communicating his word through dreams.'[2] The story of Joseph and Pharaoh is worth studying in this regard. Prophecy should not merely be thought of as telling the future; rather it is telling forth God's message. In that sense, all preachers ought to be prophets as they declare the unsearchable riches of Christ.

Many of the prophets spoke of their writings as visions (see Isa. 1:1; Obad. 1). In Numbers 12:6 God had stated, 'When a prophet of the LORD is among you, I reveal myself to him in visions, I speak to him in dreams.' Luther tells us that 'prophesying, visions and dreams are all one thing.'[3] Prophesy is making God known, so John Stott concludes that 'in that sense all God's people are now prophets, just as all are also priests and kings'.[4]

The Messianic kingdom (vv. 30–32)

These are signs that the last days have commenced. In Acts 2, Peter interpreted Joel's word 'afterwards' as 'the last days' (Acts 2:17). He was indicating to the crowds in Jerusalem that the Messianic age had finally arrived, and the pouring out of God's Holy Spirit was the positive sign of it. O. Palmer Robertson put it like this: 'The world does not have to wait any longer for the rule of Christ to begin. The outpouring of the Spirit by the Messianic king in fulfilment of Joel's prophecy indicates that the kingdom has come. The Day of the Lord has arrived with the exaltation of the Messianic Lord to his kingly throne.'[5]

The first of these signs to be mentioned are the great wonders that will be shown in the sky. During his earthly ministry Jesus spoke about the coming destruction of Jerusalem but he applied it to the day of the Lord. He spoke about this final day of punishment when 'There will be great earthquakes, famines and pestilences … fearful events and great signs from heaven' (Luke 21:11). The moon being turned to blood speaks of the trouble and bloodshed that will accompany the final judgement of this world. Zephaniah speaks of blood being 'poured out like dust' (Zeph. 1:17). There will be great destruction on that day, the aftermath of war and burning cities.

The world is in chaos today, just as it was at the beginning. Fighting and wars abound with regularity and men's hearts are failing them for fear (see Luke 21:26). Yet the Lord has promised that there will be deliverance, but it is to be found only on Mount Zion and in Jerusalem (v. 32). The closing verses of Obadiah's prophecy describe similar events and also state that those who flee to this holy mountain will be saved.[6]

So what hope is there for those of us who are not Jews and who do not live in Jerusalem or Judah? There is much hope, because 'everyone who calls on the name of the LORD will be saved', and it is on Mount Zion and in Jerusalem that salvation will be experienced. What does Joel mean by Mount Zion and Jerusalem? He is talking about God's dwelling place. We know that 'the Most High does not live in houses made by men' (Acts 7:48), and in Galatians 4:25–26 Paul speaks about Jerusalem and says that it is 'above' and is 'free'. This means that anyone can come to God (i.e. to Mount Zion and Jerusalem). None will be turned away, and if we sincerely call upon the name of the Lord, we will find that the Lord will call us and we will be delivered.

FOR FURTHER STUDY

1. Trace the Holy Spirit's activity in the Old Testament (see, for example, Gen. 1:2; 6:3; Num. 11:17, 25–26; 11:18; Deut. 34:9; 2 Kings 2:9, 15). What do we learn about the Holy Spirit?
2. How did God communicate through dreams in the Old Testament? See Genesis 28:12–15; 37:5–10; 40:1–41:40; 1 Kings 3:5–15; Daniel 2.

TO THINK ABOUT AND DISCUSS

1. The three things that God told Micah that his people need to do are 'to act justly and to love mercy and to walk humbly with [their] God' (Micah 6:8). Why do you think that humility is listed as a spiritual virtue? (See 2 Kings 22:19; Ps. 34:18; 51:17; Isa. 57:15; 1 Peter 5:5–6.) How do you match up to these requirements?
2. What does it mean to call on the name of the Lord? See Genesis 4:26; 12:8; Psalm 116:17; Zephaniah 3:9. Do you call on the name of the Lord?

10 The nations judged

(3:1–8)

When the surrounding heathen nations saw the devastation wrought upon Judah by the locust swarms, they laughed. Joel was especially hurt by their taunts when they jeered, 'Where is your God now?' (see 2:17). Those who serve the Lord often have to suffer derision from the ungodly people around them.

The Israelites endured the pains of slavery in Egypt for many years—but then God heard their cries and sent them a deliverer in the form of Moses. Indeed, throughout their long history, when they were persecuted they cried out to their God, 'How long, O Lord?' (see Ps. 35:17).

God hears the cry of his people (vv. 1–3)

God will not leave his people to suffer for ever. The people must have been feeling very disillusioned, but Joel gave them good news. God's promise was that 'in those days and at that time' they would be vindicated. However, he did not say that they would see justice done immediately. He spoke about this coming to pass 'in those days'. This phrase obviously refers to the time when God would 'pour out [his] Spirit on all people' (2:28). We have already seen that, according to Acts 2:17, these are 'the last days' which began at Pentecost and will continue right up until the final last day—the day of the Lord when the Lord Jesus Christ will return in great judgement.

Once again, the Lord restated his promise of restoration that he made at 2:25. He spoke about the time when he would 'restore the fortunes of Judah and Jerusalem'. He further promised that there would be a time when the injustices of the past would be put right. He was speaking about the boastful nations around Judah who would one day meet their match. On that day, God would 'bring them down to the Valley of Jehoshaphat' and there he would 'enter into judgment against them'. Joel referred to this particular valley again at 3:12 and we can see from verse 14 that it was 'the valley of decision'; not 'a' valley of decision, but 'the special valley where a powerful decision is made'.

It would appear that Joel was referring to a valley which lay somewhere near Jerusalem, but the spot cannot be identified with any certainty. Tradition says that it was either the Valley of Hinnom or, more likely, the Kidron Valley. The important point was that it was the valley of judgement. The name Jehoshaphat means 'the Lord judges'. The situation highlighted by Joel here is similar to that described by the Lord Jesus Christ in the parable of the sheep and the goats (Matt. 25:31–46). That parable refers to the time 'when the

Son of Man comes in his glory, and all the angels with him' and relates to a trial of all the nations who will be 'gathered before him' (Matt. 25:31–32). These nations will be judged on the basis of how they treated the Lord and his brothers.

Although God had punished Judah by sending the devastating locusts, he still referred to them as 'my inheritance, my people Israel' and to the area as 'my land' (3:2). These heathen nations had swooped down and scattered God's people among the nations and divided up the sacred land of Israel. Elizabeth Achtemeier writes, 'When foreigners took portions of Israel's land, they were therefore robbing God's possession, and they stand guilty before God for that usurpation.'[1] The land had been promised to Israel, but the writer of Lamentations sobbed, 'Our inheritance has been turned over to aliens, our homes to foreigners' (Lam. 5:2).

The scattering of 'my people' is likely to refer to the Babylonian deportation in 597 and 589 BC. The nations around treated God's people as though they were of little value. They cast lots for them so that the boys were traded for prostitution and the girls were sold similarly in exchange for wine—the drinking of which would only bring them pleasure until the effects of the alcohol wore off.

The tables turned against the heathen nations (vv. 4–8)

The poetry which Joel has so far employed now turns abruptly to stark prose as the Lord turned his attention to the fate of two groups of people who lived to the west of Jerusalem. To the north-west were the proud Phoenicians, specifically the people of Tyre and Sidon, and the lands of Philistia were situated to the east and south. In effect, the Lord said to these people, 'Who do you think you are? Do you think you have the right to "get your own back" against me?'

Then the Lord stopped hinting and spoke of specific action: 'I will swiftly and speedily return on your own heads what you have done' (v. 4). Punishment would not be delayed and there would be no opportunity for these ungodly people to 'mend their ways'. They had invaded Judah when they had the opportunity. They had quickly and selfishly taken some of the silver and gold ornaments from God's temple in Jerusalem and carried them back to decorate their own temples, which were dedicated to heathen gods, who were no gods at all. They assumed that they could get away with such evil behaviour. However, their greater crime was much more serious than taking material things: they had stolen and then sold the people of Judah and Jerusalem to the Greeks. This had been happening from as early as 800 BC.[2]

Amos spoke of God's abhorrence of slavery; God warned that he would 'send fire upon the walls of Tyre that will consume her fortresses' because 'she sold whole communities of captives to Edom' (Amos 1:9–10). The Philistines had been in the habit of behaving in the same way. In fact, they had been a thorn in the side of Judah from the days of the judges (see Judg. 13:1), during the time of Samuel (1 Sam. 5:1) and the reign of Jehoram (2 Chr. 21:16–17). Ezekiel 25:15–17 mentions a whole catalogue of their sins. This enmity among the peoples in that area of the world has continued right into the 21st century.

So what would God do about such dreadful behaviour? Sometimes the Lord allows people to remain in their sin and so suffer the consequences of it (see 1 Kings 8:31–32; Jer. 50:29; Hab. 2:8; Matt. 18:23–35; Rev. 18:4–17). This behaviour breeds 'hatred for hatred', and we can see examples of this from secular history and in our daily news media reports. But in the case of the sins of Tyre, Sidon and Philistia, God acted and returned to them what they had done. The children of these nations were going to be sold to the people of Judah, who would then sell them to the Sabeans, the people of Sheba (Joel 3:8). We know that the queen of Sheba visited King Solomon (1 Kings 10:1–13), but the land itself is not identified in Scripture. All we know is that it was a 'nation far away'. Jeremiah also tells us that it was 'a distant land' (Jer. 6:20). Archaeology suggests that it was located in the south-western part of the Arabian Peninsula which is now Yeman. However, the point that God was making was that Sheba was in the exact opposite direction from Greece.

We see, then, that principles of justice are displayed here. God would return the deeds of these heathen nations upon their own heads. In Scripture we see that the crimes of wrongdoers come back upon them; retribution is a biblical truth (see Ps. 7:14–15; Prov. 26:27).

FOR FURTHER STUDY

1. Study the prayers of God's people in the following passages: Exodus 5:22–23; Numbers 11:10–17; Joshua 7:1–26; Psalm 6:2; 35:17–18. What can we learn about how we can pray to God? You may find it helpful to read *How Long, O Lord?* by D. A. Carson (Leicester: IVP, 1990).

2. How does God respond to confessed sin? See Psalm 103:12; Isaiah 1:18; 38:17; 43:25; Jeremiah 31:34; 50:20; Micah 7:18–19. You may find it helpful to read *Revolutionary Forgiveness* by Eric E. Wright (Darlington: Evangelical Press, 2002).

3. It is easy to have a 'holier than thou' attitude towards those who are disobedient to the Lord, but note what God says about people with such an attitude in Isaiah 65:5b. Dwell on the advice of Paul in Philippians 4:8.

TO THINK ABOUT AND DISCUSS

1. Consider the lives of those Bible characters who had to spend many years waiting for God's deliverance—for example, Joseph, David and Jeremiah. What can we learn from them about our own lives?

2. Think back to a time when someone treated you badly. How did you respond? Read Matthew 5:39; John 13:34; Romans 12:10; 1 Peter 1:22. How should we respond to situations like this? Do you find this easy?

11 Prepare for war

(3:9–16)

As the people of Judah listened to Joel's call to repent, they must have realized that the day of the Lord would not be an easy one for them. However, the call to prepare for war in this section was not addressed to the people of Judah, but to the surrounding nations (see vv. 9a, 11a). Joel called on each nation to prepare for war.

First he called them to wake up out of their sleepy lethargy; their warriors were to 'rouse' themselves (vv. 9, 12). Joel had already used this word in connection with the Judeans who had been sold into slavery, when God said through him, 'I am going to rouse them out of the places to which you sold them' (v. 7). Now, in verse 9, he called 'all the fighting men [to] draw near and attack'.

Joel speaks (vv. 9–11)

No one would be excused from this battle; even the weak and feeble needed to be armed and were to declare, 'I am strong!' 'Even the physically weak and psychologically unsuited are not to be exempted.'[1]

Then Joel reversed the instructions given by Isaiah and Micah (see Isa. 2:4; Micah 4:3). Unlike the coming times of peace and prosperity they foretold, Joel warned the nations to be ready to fight, as God would put wrongs to right. In verse 7 the Lord had promised that the slaves would go home and those who perpetrated iniquities against them would be punished in a way that suited their crime. In verses 9–10 these same heathen nations were to transform their agricultural implements into weapons of warfare.

Joel next advised them to be united. This was not going to be a time for each of these nations to stand alone; they were all to act, and were to do so quickly. Then Joel turned to God and told him that everyone was ready for the battle, shouting with a great voice, 'Bring down your warriors, O LORD!' (v. 11).

The day of the Lord will be dreadful. Joel gives us a number of descriptions of it. In 2:10–11 he spoke of the earth shaking, the sky trembling, the sun and moon being darkened and the stars ceasing to shine as the Lord thunders in full voice at the head of his army. The day of the Lord will be 'great' and 'dreadful'; 'Who can endure it?' In 2:30–31 we read about the 'wonders in the heavens and on the earth': 'blood and fire and billows of smoke'. 'The sun will be turned to darkness and the moon to blood before the coming of the ... day of the LORD.' But we also see the Lord's gracious mercy being extended, as 'everyone who calls on the name of the LORD will be saved'.

God speaks (vv. 12–16)

Once again we read about the Valley of Jehoshaphat (see 3:2). The heathen nations would be roused from the complacency which had come upon them as a result of their power over the people of Judah and Jerusalem. They had assumed that they were still in control of events, but now they would need to move forward into the Valley of Jehoshaphat where decisive events would take place. An army, a nation or an individual caught in a valley is in a vulnerable position because there are few places to hide; the enemy can look down from both sides and trap them in a pincer movement. This valley would be the place where God would 'judge all the nations on every side' (v. 12). The Lord God Almighty, whose honour these nations had impugned, would sit and do his work of judgement.

The Lord spoke in terms that the people would understand, using agricultural language. When the corn is ripe, the farmer swings his sickle to cut down the wheat and so gather the richly swollen grains. When the owner of the vineyard sees that his grapes are ripe and full of juice, he picks them and loads them into the winepress where the heavy weights can squeeze out every last drop of liquid, so that the vats overflow with their blood-red fluid.

> The farmer knows when his crops are ripe and ready to harvest; God is the same.

The farmer knows when his crops are ripe and ready to harvest;

God is the same. On the day of the Lord, these nations will be ready for judgement—'so great is their wickedness!' (v. 13). This judgement will be great and it will be final. There will be no escape from it for those who fail to repent and turn to Christ. There will be 'multitudes, multitudes' moaning and groaning in the valley of decision (v. 14), only it will not be their decision now, but the Lord's. These heathen people made their decision when they chose to turn against the Lord and his Anointed.

On that dreadful day, 'The sun and moon will be darkened, and the stars no longer shine. The LORD will roar from Zion and thunder from Jerusalem; the earth and the sky will tremble.' Amos speaks of the Lord roaring like a lion as he comes in judgement upon evildoers (Amos 1:2). Darkness, sorrow and gloom are the lot of those who reject the Lord God Almighty. Jesus speaks of this judgement as outer darkness: there shall be 'weeping and gnashing of teeth' (Matt. 8:12).

There is hope for everyone (v. 16b)

The Bible speaks of places of refuge. When the children of Israel entered the Promised Land, the Lord provided cities of refuge for those who were in trouble (see Josh. 20). Those being pursued by avenging family members of people they had unintentionally wronged could hide in these cities and be kept safe until they stood trial. Psalm 46, with its reminder that God is the refuge and strength of his people, has given great comfort to many, particularly during times of great danger. Isaiah speaks of the Lord as being a refuge 'for the poor' and 'for the needy in his distress' (Isa. 25:4).

Despite God's just and justifiable judgement against sin and sinners, he has provided a refuge for his people. Those who come to the Lord Jesus Christ in sincere and genuine repentance and trust will find that he is a stronghold for them. They will be as safe from the wrath of God when he brings judgement upon this world as were those eight people in the ark when the storms beat upon it (Gen. 7:23).

FOR FURTHER STUDY

1. Read Matthew 13:40–42; 25:46; Romans 14:10–12; 2 Corinthians 5:10. What do we learn from these verses about God's judgement on the last day?
2. How does the Bible liken God's judgement to a harvest? See Jeremiah 25:30–31; Hosea 6:11; Matthew 13:39; Revelation 14:15–19.

TO THINK ABOUT AND DISCUSS

1. Do you warn your unsaved friends about the judgement of the last day? Read Romans 14:10–12; 2 Corinthians 5:10. How can you help your friends to take this seriously?
2. How should we seek to lead to Christ a person who has lived an outwardly wicked life?

12 Blessings for ever

(3:17–21)

So many people are living such troubled lives that they turn to drugs or a whole range of pleasures, or simply fill their ears with music from their MP3 players. They live in uncertainty because of financial, heath or relationship problems. They have little peace in their lives; some even commit suicide because of their loneliness.

No doubt many of the people of Judah in Joel's day were also filled with trouble; but when they repented, God assured them, 'Then you will know that I, the LORD your God, dwell in Zion, my holy hill' (v. 17).

They would be certain of this when they saw evidence of God's blessing on their material lives. They had felt pain when his hand of judgement came upon them and their fields were ruined by the onslaughts of the locusts (see 1:10). They were in despair when their harvest was ruined and all their fruit had withered and dried up (1:11–12). They had suffered when the priests were unable to offer sacrifices in the temple (1:9). But now Joel has given them good news of salvation, in both a material and a spiritual way.

The assurance that the Lord would be their refuge and their stronghold (3:16) would fill them with great joy, knowing that he was with them in the middle of their difficulties. Because God was with them, they would be prosperous. Their enemies would never afflict them again because they had been destroyed—as was the army of the Egyptians that pursued the children of Israel when they fled from Egypt (see Exod. 14:30).

The land will prosper (v. 18)

This verse starts with the phrase 'In that day'. This is the same period of time that we find at 3:1—'In those days and at that time'. The prophet continued to outline the blessings of being restored to the Lord's favour. Just as two lovers may suddenly experience a rekindling of the joy of their first love (but see Rev. 2:4), so God's people would know the return of all past favour—except that, this time, these gifts would be 'pressed down ... and running over' (see Luke 6:38).

'In that day', bountiful harvests would again be given; in fact, on the great day of the Lord there will be a triumphal time of harvest. We have already seen in 3:13 that the harvest of the wicked will be all-encompassing so that no one will escape. In that day,

> the kings of the earth, the princes, the generals, the rich, the mighty, and every slave and every free man hid in caves and among the rocks of the mountains. They called to the

mountains and the rocks, 'Fall on us and hide us from the face of him who sits on the throne and from the wrath of the Lamb! For the great day of their wrath has come, and who can stand?'

(Rev. 6:15–17)

But for the Lord's own people, who have returned to him in repentance, 'the mountains will drip new wine, and the hills will flow with milk; all the ravines of Judah will run with water' (Joel 3:18). The harvest will be so bountiful that 'A fountain will flow out of the LORD's house and will water the valley of acacias'. Amos paints a similar picture in Amos 9:13–15.

The valley of acacias is also sometimes translated 'the valley of Shittim'. This is a 'deep and rocky portion of the Kidron Valley or wadi that begins northwest of Jerusalem, bends around east of the city, and then continues through a deep gorge southeast toward the Dead Sea'.[1] The Dead Sea is a very barren area which is made up of about 25 per cent salt. Nothing lives in its waters, nor does any vegetation grow there, but amazingly acacias grew in abundance in the dry valley of Shittim during biblical times. To illustrate the great change which would come about on 'that day', Joel spoke of this dry valley as being deluged with water flowing from the Lord's house.

This abundance of material things is but a pale reflection of the great outpouring of spiritual blessings that God's blood-bought people will receive on that great day of judgement. These will be for those who know, love and serve him, but everlasting punishment will be dealt to those who are the enemies of God and who fail to respond to his entreaties to come to him and be saved. All these ungodly people are summed up under the names of two ancient nations: Egypt and Edom.

Egypt and Edom will receive their just deserts (v. 19)

The mention of water brings our thoughts to Egypt and 'the desert of trouble' passed through by the forebears of the people of Judah. The Israelites had been slaves in Egypt and placed under harsh treatment there for 400 years. While the Egyptians experienced floods of water containing the rich nutrients of the Nile, all that the Israelites experienced was a harsh drought. However, Joel explains that 'in that day' the tables would be turned. Egypt would end up as a 'desolate' place, while God's people would revel in an abundance of good things.

Edom also had behaved very badly towards Judah. The people of Edom were descended from Esau, the greedy brother of Jacob, but had refused to let the children of Israel pass through their territory when they journeyed from Egypt. Instead they made these weary pilgrims go all the way round their land before they could enter the Promised Land (Num. 20:20). Later, the people of Edom had watched and mocked while Judah's enemies had carried the Judeans away into captivity. Obadiah tells us that they had proudly 'looked down' on their brother nation and did nothing to help them (see Obad. 8–12). But on the day of the Lord, Edom, which had once boasted of its great wealth which was 'safely' hidden away in its caves, would become a 'desert waste, because of violence done to the people of Judah'.

In the garden of Eden there was also an abundance of good

things, but sin entered the world and spoiled everything. However, Joel speaks of hope, as in 'that day' there will be a new garden, and a new Jerusalem. There will be a

> river of the water of life, as clear as crystal, flowing from the throne of God and of the Lamb ... On each side of the river [will stand] the tree of life, bearing twelve crops of fruit, yielding its fruit every month. And the leaves of the tree are for the healing of the nations. No longer will there be any curse.
>
> (Rev. 22:1–3)

This is the fulfilment of Ezekiel's prophecy, in which he speaks of 'water coming out from the threshold of the temple towards the east' (see Ezek. 47:1–12).

Judah vindicated (vv. 20–21)

Even though Judah and the people of Jerusalem had not always behaved in godly ways, the Lord promised to lavish great blessings upon them 'in that day'. He will do the same to everyone who has heeded his call to repent and has turned to him. Isaiah issued the Lord's call for his people to come to him and be washed so that they would be 'as white as snow' (Isa. 1:18). However, that blessed state could not come to full fruition until God's only Son, the Lord Jesus Christ, offered up his sinless life upon the cross of Calvary. There he paid the price of the sin of all who come to him in repentance and faith. 'On that day a fountain will be opened to the house of David and the inhabitants of Jerusalem, to cleanse them from sin and impurity' (Zech. 13:1). This offer of mercy is opened to all the inhabitants of Jerusalem: '... the Holy City, the new Jerusalem, coming down out of heaven from God, prepared as a bride beautifully dressed for her husband'. John tells us that the 'dwelling of God [will be] with men, and he will live with them. They will be his people, and God himself will be with them and be their God' (Rev. 21:2–3).

The Lord does not leave his people in any doubt about their salvation. If we wonder whether our sins have been so vile that the Lord cannot forgive them, Joel gives us a positive response. He said of Judah, 'Their bloodguilt, which I have not pardoned, I will pardon' (v. 21). There is much discussion about the precise meaning of this phrase; the King James Version renders it as 'I will cleanse their blood'. Leslie Allen enters into a full discussion on the various possible meanings,[2] but Calvin explains that it means that God's people will be cleansed so that there will be no possibility of any further judgement coming upon them.[3] And what was true for the people of Judah then is true for anyone today who repents of his or her sins and turns to Christ for salvation.

The prophecy ends with this bold and definite statement: 'The LORD dwells in Zion!' Whatever danger, problem or anxiety the Lord's people may fear or experience, they can be certain of this: God is still on the throne, and those who dwell with him will be kept safe and secure.

So Joel ends his short prophecy with the message of deliverance for God's people. Those who doubt the truth of these promises need only remember that 'the LORD dwells in Zion'. As he dwells and reigns there, God's people, who are citizens of heaven, will dwell with him, 'in the house of the LORD for ever' (Ps. 23:6).

For further study ▶

FOR FURTHER STUDY

1. Study Exodus 25:8; 1 Kings 8:12–13; Psalm 68:16, 18; Isaiah 8:18; Ezekiel 43:9. What does it mean for God to dwell in Zion, among his people?
2. God promised to Israel a land flowing with milk and honey. How this will be ultimately fulfilled in the new Jerusalem (see Ps. 46:4; Rev. 22:1–2).

TO THINK ABOUT AND DISCUSS

1. The 18th-century hymn-writer William Cowper often found he was in a 'dry' place spiritually. Following one of these experiences, he wrote his famous hymn 'O For a Closer Walk with God'. In the second verse he pleaded with the Lord,

> Where is the blessedness I knew,
> When first I saw the Lord?
> Where is the soul-refreshing view
> Of Jesus and his Word?

Have you had an experience like this? How did you return to the Lord?

2. God's promise of prosperity does not always result in material blessing. Do you know of Christians who are poor in terms of this world's goods but who have an abundance of spiritual riches? You may know them personally, or you may only have heard about them.

OPENING UP JOEL

Commentary on Hosea, Joel, Amos, Obadiah and Jonah, p. 242.
3 Quoted in John Stott, *The Message of Acts* (Leicester: IVP, 1990), p. 74.
4 Stott, *The Message of Acts,* p. 74.
5 Robertson, *Prophet of the Coming Day of the Lord,* p. 85.
6 For further, more detailed explanation, see my commentary on Hosea and Obadiah: *Turning Back to God* (Darlington: Evangelical Press, 2001), pp. 245–250.

Chapter 10
1 Achtemeier, *Minor Prophets,* p. 153.
2 *NIV Study Bible* ([n.p.]: Zondervan, 1987), p. 1322.

Chapter 11
1 Leslie C. Allen, *The Books of Joel, Obadiah, Jonah and Micah* (New International Commentary on the Old Testament; Grand Rapids, MI: Eerdmans, 1976), p. 115.

Chapter 12
1 Achtemeier, *Minor Prophets,* p. 160
2 Allen, p. 117.
3 John Calvin, *A Commentary on the Prophet Joel* (London: Banner of Truth, 1958), pp. 131–132.

Endnotes

Chapter 1
1 See bbc.co.uk/schools/religion/judaism/passover.shtml.
2 Thomas J. Finley, *Joel, Obadiah and Micah* (Chicago: Moody Press, 1996), p. 26.

Chapter 2
1 Lloyd J. Ogilvie, *The Communicator's Commentary on Hosea, Joel, Amos, Obadiah and Jonah* (Dallas: Word, 1990), p. 213.

Chapter 3
1 Elizabeth Achtemeier, *Minor Prophets*, vol. i (New International Biblical Commentary; Carlisle: Paternoster, 1996), p. 126.

Chapter 4
1 Ibid, p. 132.

Chapter 5
1 Ibid.
2 Finley, *Joel, Obadiah and Micah*, p. 32.
3 Achtemeier, *Minor Prophets*, pp. 130–131.
4 Ibid.

Chapter 6
1 Michael Bentley, *Opening Up*
2 Ogilvie, *The Communicator's*
Concordia, 1956), p. 128.

Chapter 7
1 John Murray, *Redemption Accomplished and Applied* (Edinburgh: Banner of Truth, 1961), p. 114.
2 Anthony Selvaggio, *The Prophets Speak of Him* (Darlington: Evangelical Press, 2006), p. 33.
3 Finley, *Joel, Obadiah and Micah*, p. 45.

Chapter 8
1 O. Palmer Robertson, *Prophet of the Coming Day of the Lord: The Message of Joel* (Darlington: Evangelical Press, 1995), p. 64.
2 The Hebrew translated 'autumn rains in righteousness' can also be translated 'the teacher for righteousness'. For a detailed discussion of these two variations, see Robertson, *Prophet of the Coming Day of the Lord*, pp. 69–73.
3 Robertson, *Prophet of the Coming Day of the Lord*, p. 77.

Chapter 9
1 Theo Laetsch, *The Minor Prophets* (St Louis, MO: Concordia, 1956), p. 128.
2 Ogilvie, *The Communicator's*

Zephaniah (Leominster: Day One, 2008), p. 37.